WOLF MASKS

Under severe moons he sits making
Wolf-masks, mouths clamped well onto the world.
                        Ted Hughes, "February"

Kennikat Press
National University Publications
Literary Criticism Series

General Editor
John E. Becker
Fairleigh Dickinson University

LAWRENCE R. RIES

WOLF MASKS

VIOLENCE IN CONTEMPORARY POETRY

821.
914
RIES

National University Publications
KENNIKAT PRESS   //   1977
Port Washington, N. Y.   //   London

78-05468

Manufactured in the United States of America

Published by
Kennikat Press Corp.
Port Washington, N. Y./London

Library of Congress Cataloging in Publication Data

Ries, Lawrence R.
    Wolf masks.

    (National university publications: Literary
criticism series)
    Bibliography: p.
    Includes index.
    1. English poetry—20th century—History and
criticism. 2. Violence in literature. I. Title.
PR508.V55R5   821'.9'1409   76-30540
ISBN 0-8046-9168-1

CONTENTS

To Madelaine

PREFACE

There are both great rewards and great risks in approaching our contemporaries. We do not have to transport ourselves through time in order to share their environment, nor have their voices had time to grow crusty or golden with age. Reputations have not yet hardened so that we are prevented from seeing more than one aspect of the artist's work. When we read his poem, we frequently find ourselves nodding thoughtfully in agreement, not necessarily because we understand what he is saying but because we *know* the sources and causes of his expression; we have been there ourselves.

But because the stature that time and critics have thrust upon the writers of past centuries does not tower over us, there is also the temptation to be too casual with these poets. Philip Larkin has told us that the poet today might very well be our next-door neighbor, and can we really trust and respect him? And to meet the poet face to face . . . the concept of artist reduces itself to shady reality before our eyes. It becomes even more important to keep our eyes on the tale, not the teller. Then there is the problem of unexplored territory. Most of the poets whom I discuss in the following pages had little or no reputation when I began my study. Ten years ago a critic could have written almost anything about any one of these poets, and while it might not have been correct, it had a good chance of being fresh and new.

It was a strange and discomforting experience to watch reputations flower before my eyes and then change hues. Thom Gunn was considered if not the best young poet at least the one with the greatest potential in the late fifties and early sixties. He may not need a full reintroduction to the intellectual community, but he has certainly not assumed the position he seemed destined for. On the other hand, it has been difficult to keep up

1

with the many critical and biographical pieces that keep appearing on Sylvia Plath. Not only have her work and life been scrutinized in their smallest details, but there is that additional problem of trying to keep one's critical ship sailing according to what he feels to be the real currents of her poetry rather than being drawn off course by those voices that have prematurely enshrined this poet. The real temptation is to give in to the pressures of biographical criticism; but the warnings are clear, since there are too many examples of those who, in the quest after the myth of Sylvia Plath, have abandoned her art. Her poetry is a solid achievement, and we can pay it the greatest respect by not distorting it through romanticized hindsight.

Finally, my greatest regret is that I have had to deal with partial *opera.* Three of the four poets under discussion in the following pages are still actively productive, and their careers are by no means static, as the printed page often makes them appear. Even while this manuscript was in various stages of editing, new volumes of poetry were appearing: *Season Songs,* by Ted Hughes, and *Feng* by John Wain. There is no guarantee that the conclusions drawn today will not be only partial truths tomorrow. In our devotion to contemporary poetry, we hope the artist will always be several turns in front of the critic, and even in those moments when we think we finally "have him," we know we only have one of his elusive selves, while his other masks are disappearing into the maze of his art.

I am deeply grateful to my fellow explorers, those critics who are working in areas of contemporary literature that receive little examination. They have been helpful, both when I have leaned on them, but equally so when I have kicked against their goad. I owe special thanks to Edmond Epstein, who so expertly led me into the world of the contemporary poem; he and Ted Boyle offered a great deal of advice in the early stages of this work. I wish also to acknowledge gratefully a grant from the Research Foundation of the State University of New York.

Lawrence R. Ries

State University of New York
at Albany

1

LITERATURE AND VIOLENCE

The inner world of vision and the outer world of society have waged continual battle for the British poet's loyalty through the centuries.[1] A liberal humanism that began with Chaucer and followed in an oblique line to Matthew Arnold has been the primary force in uniting these two worlds; in easing this tension, however, the poet frequently found himself in the position of reinforcing the structure of society through his poetry. Although frequently a critic of the world he inhabited, the poet nevertheless saw it as his role to prepare others to live in that world. Spenser announced that the purpose of *The Faerie Queene* was "to fashion a gentleman or noble person in vertuous and gentle discipline."[2] Matthew Arnold, envisioning a somewhat wider role for poetry, predicted that "most of what now passes with us for religion and philosophy will be replaced by poetry."[3] But it was in Arnold's time that the separation between the inner and outer world was becoming a hostile breach, represented initially by the pre-Raphaelite Brotherhood and later more dramatically by the Decadents. The trials of Whistler and Wilde were visible evidence of the irreconcilable differences between the artist and society, with society taking a dim view of the artist's attempt to assert either aesthetic or moral freedom from its own standards. This dichotomy between the inner and outer world established a pattern for the basic movements of twentieth-century British poetry, a dichotomy that increases in tension as the century progresses.

The split between the poet's vision and his environment has not proved very productive for his art. From the pre-Raphaelites and Decadents, who were true to their vision, to Newbolt, Kipling, and Roy Campbell, who were true to their countries, there was no truly great poetry. The two greatest poets of the period, Eliot and Yeats, had to rise above this division to find workable metaphors in systems that transcended both the poet and society. Auden's transformation from political propagandist to metaphysical seer can also be seen as an attempt to reach beyond the limitations established by the schism described above.

These limitations still appear to be the greatest obstacle to the writing of poetry in the era following World War II. Even more than in the early part of the century, the insensitivity and cruelty of the world have forced the poet into a private corner from which he finds it difficult to emerge. One solution, perhaps the simplest, would be for him to sit there and bemoan the loss of values that has so offended his sensitivity. But the greater, the more difficult duty before him is to reconcile the inner and outer world, to evaluate the experience of the war and the struggle for power that followed, and to come to terms with the world he must now live in. Robert Conquest in a tone of desperate hope expressed his awareness of the difficulties facing the poet in the wake of World War II:

> For I must believe
> That somewhere the poet is working who can handle
> The flung world and his own heart. To him I say
> The little I can. I offer him the debris
> Of five years; undirected storm in self and Europe,
> And my love. Let him take it for what it's worth.[4]

There are, in retrospect, a number of poets to whom these lines might have been addressed, for after the war many poets were concerned with, and attempted to come to terms with, the violence, both physical and psychological, that they saw as the characteristic quality of the world in which they found themselves.

In preparing this study my concern has not been to catalogue all those poets who have written poems on the subject of violence. I have chosen the individual rather than the panoramic approach, and in doing so I have attempted to concentrate on those poets whose philosophical and metaphysical concerns are serious enough to expose, under exacting scrutiny, stimulating, challenging insights into ourselves and into our physical and psychological environment. This approach, exclusive as it is, suffers in many ways. It fails, for example, to exhibit a broad scope of contemporary poetry, by limiting itself to poets who are aesthetically and intellectually distinctive. As a result of this limitation, the sensibility and refinement of the poets I discuss may remove them too far from the world of common feeling to make them seem truly representative in the way that I want them to be. But after considering such arguments, I still felt that what is lost in scope is gained in depth of vision, and that the points of view represented by the poets under discussion are sufficiently broad to be inclusive of or parallel to most other poets of the same generation.

The four poets whose reactions to violence are studied here are Sylvia Plath, Thom Gunn, Ted Hughes, and John Wain. All are British except for Plath, an American who studied and lived in England and who married the British poet Ted Hughes. In addition to their concern with violence, which links them, these poets shared growth to maturity shortly before and during the war. Poets of an earlier vintage—Auden, Barker, Graves, and others who still wrote after the war—were by no means left unaffected by the increasing violence of the world; however, the multiple influences upon their development are too diverse to be isolated in the present manner. It was the younger poets to whom Conquest offered the debris of the "storm in self and Europe" with the hope that they might approach it with a newly formed sensitivity, with new initiative.

A further problem in scope is to define what we mean by violence. Because the twentieth century has witnessed such extensive violence, and because not only the news media but sociologists, historians, and psychologists have made man so conscious of his destructive potentiality, the term has become rather amorphous. I use the term "violence" in two basic senses, somewhat generalized but sufficiently directed and inclusive for my purposes. The first kind of violence is that injury, whether physical or psychological, that man inflicts upon his fellow man. The second is the spontaneous and powerful energy which belongs to the natural order; although this force may be terrible and dangerous, it is also a source of life.

For any action to be considered violent in the first sense, it would seem necessary that it be harmful to human life. While this may be a broad description, it immediately demonstrates the part that judgment plays in establishing an act as violent. If an ignorant person were to witness a man being tortured and a man undergoing surgery, he would perhaps be unable to distinguish the purpose of these acts. But the surgeon's intention is not to harm the patient; it is quite the contrary. The torturer, of course, has no such high purpose. Even those who would justify the purpose of the torturer, or to take a clearer example, of the executioner, would not deny that human harm is involved. These people would presumably argue that, in spite of the harm involved, the violence is justified.

It is clear that any consideration of this kind of violence involves a strong moral judgment. One of the common assumptions underlying its very definition is that whatever harms man is wrong. This moral proposition may be extended to include harm to those things which delight man, such as his possessions, works of art, and so on. In responding to violence of this nature, whether it be to defend it or to attack it, people generally act from deep moral commitments.

The most obvious form that such violence takes is physical. It is most visible in the personal criminal act, such as murder, robbery, rape. But most people find this violence more disturbing in its larger sociological expression: warfare, riots, ecological disaster, genocide. Man's moral sense can dismiss the individual act as an aberration, but the socially acceptable or at least socially justifiable act of violence is more difficult to condone. Attempts to understand and reconcile such acts are evident in the voluminous reports by commissions on violence, and in the published studies of collective violence by sociologists and psychologists. If only man could understand this expression of violence, they seem to say, if only he could uncover the logic of such events, he would be able to grasp truths about human life that, once known, would not eliminate the tragic from our experience but would make it more bearable and perhaps shift the level of tragedy from the social to the cosmic.

The violence that involves not only individuals but entire classes of people or entire societies finds a more destructive and dangerous expression in its psychological form. The violence that touches few people physically can affect millions more merely through their being aware of it. Modern communication media can transform a private or local act of violence into a national or international experience. Certainly, a recent event such as the shootout between the Symbionese Liberation Army and federal officers produced tensions and conflict that could not have been so extensive without the news media. Two events whose psychological effects have been even more pervasive (because they are less localized) are the atomic bomb scare in the 1950s and the present awareness of ecological imbalance. Perhaps the strongest psychological force is that violence which hides behind ordered government, the laws of society, and peaceful citizens, the kind of violence of which Thomas Merton accuses the wealthy nations of the world:

When a system can, without resort to overt force, compel people to live in conditions of abjection, helplessness, wretchedness that keep them on a level of beasts rather than men, it is plainly violent. To make men live on a subhuman level, to constrain them in such a way that they have no hope of escaping their condition, is an unjust exercise of force. Those who in some way or other concur in that oppression—and profit by it—are exercising violence even though they may be preaching pacifism. And their supposed peaceful laws, which maintain this spurious kind of order, are in fact instruments of violence.[5]

The violence produced by these conditions is greater than its physical counterpart, for it produces in the individual a feeling of paralysis, a sense of impotency in regard to his own response. Because physical violence must be located in space and time, it can be understood and accepted. But psychological violence which evades such definition frequently produces uncontrollable fear and paranoia.

Such violence might broadly be termed human violence, in contrast to natural violence. The central problem of Sylvia Plath and John Wain is that their vision is limited solely to human violence without the advantage of making distinctions between the social and the cosmic that a broader perspective would provide. Sylvia Plath indeed grapples with the forces of violence described here, but her battle is waged so intensely that she is never able to free herself to see beyond these forces. Wain appears to be intimidated and refuses to join battle. Rather than pass through the knowledge of injurious violence to deeper understanding, he is overcome by the psychological threat and refuses to involve himself with this subject. The timidity of his response is perhaps one of the best examples of the harm done by these psychological forces.

Natural violence, on the other hand, springs from primal energy and touches man insofar as he partakes of the powerful forces in nature. Such violence is as often a source of strength and creativity as of destruction. The violent act of this kind is most often found removed from social situations; it is the act of a Van Gogh rather than of an Eichmann. The passionate pride of King Lear is an expression of this force; the same uncontrollable passions that enabled him to rule successfully in earlier years led to his downfall in old age. The strong moral undertones are missing from such acts, for the latter are parallel to spontaneous powerful thunderstorms which, though terrible, are also necessary and productive.

While the physical and psychological violence described earlier belongs to and grows out of particular social conditions, the primal, explosive forces of natural violence are universal. I believe that virtually all the poetry written after World War II that concerns itself with violence received its impetus from the perception of human violence, those immediate historical conditions that weighed so heavily upon the artist's sensitivity. Poets such as Plath, Wain, and George MacBeth were unable to transcend the human violence in order to understand the natural. Sylvia Plath made the attempt, but this attempt ended in confusion, anger, and frustration. Wain, the neo-humanist, does not attempt to come to an understanding of violence, and it is this intellectual failure that precedes his poetic failure.

On the other hand, Ted Hughes and Thom Gunn move almost immediately to a concern with natural violence. They do not avoid the issues raised by the war, but their approach is philosophical rather than empirical or moral, for they detach their poetry from immediate social concerns in order to attempt to understand the broader sources and implications of violence. Because they are at least partly successful in elevating this subject from the social level to the universal, their poetry has an emphatic note of acceptance and reconciliation rather than rejection and negation. And it is readily apparent that they are most successful poetically when they are able to keep the two senses of violence distinct.

The problem, of course, arises that it is not always possible to keep the two kinds of violence apart. What, for instance, happens when natural violence finds expression through institutional forms, such as the oppression of citizens by established governments, the killing of millions in war? Some ideologues, like Fanon, and even Yeats, attempt to justify such violence by asserting that the destructiveness of war, civil and national, is a desirable catharsis. It is perhaps easy to accept or at least to make some compromise with the abstract principles of violence that Gunn and Hughes expound, but the problem becomes somewhat more complicated when Gunn praises unthinking activists or Hughes eulogizes a dictatorial army colonel. Their failure in these instances is most probably the reason that these two poets have been extremely careful in maintaining an impersonal tone in their poetry. And while they are the most successful of the contemporary poets in discussing violence, their inability to reconcile the immediate historical situation with their philosophical principles signals a deficiency in their total vision if not in their poetry itself.

In order to understand the different ways in which the postwar poets respond to violence, it is perhaps best to review quickly the immediate historical background. The most obvious debris of the war that Robert Conquest offered to the younger poets was the destruction of millions of human beings, the ruins of a desecrated Europe, and, what was worse, the distorted sensibility born in those who witnessed the death and violence of the war. While civilization, in return for its efforts at destruction, inherited the newly released energy of the atom, the abuse of power that was associated with Nazi Germany passed to the political shoulders of both the right and the left. Without acknowledging the debt, the new world powers had adopted a principle of power directly from the man they had deposed: "Man has become great through struggle. The first fundamental of any rational Weltanschauung is the fact that on earth and in the universe force alone is decisive. Whatever good man has reached is due to his originality plus his brutality."[6]

As Hannah Arendt notes in her study of violence, this new concept of power is different from traditional power that rested upon a mutual trust and respect between the rulers and the ruled: "Power and violence are opposites; where the one rules absolutely, the other is absent. Violence appears where power is in jeopardy, but left to its own cause it ends in power's disappearance."[7] The modern crisis is that there is little reciprocity between state and citizen, and the loss of traditional power results in governance through violence: " . . . the current equation of violence with power rests on government's being understood as domination of man over man by means of violence. . . . Politically speaking, the point is that loss of power becomes a temptation to substitute violence for power. . . ."[8]

The power then that descended from Nazi Germany and Fascist Italy and infected countries like the United States, Soviet Russia, France, and England after the war was tainted by those rightist philosophies. Under these principles, power is only valuable in its employment against another:

> It is evident that the stronger has the right before God and the world to enforce his will. History shows us that right as such does not mean a thing unless it is backed up by great power. If one does not have the power to enforce his right, that right alone will profit him absolutely nothing. The stronger have always been victorious. The whole of nature is a continuous struggle between strength and weakness, and eternal victory of the strong over the weak.[9]

Under these conditions, power has become synonymous with violence rather than its opposite, and violence has become not the bizarre, the unusual, or the abhorred, but the natural, the expected, the banal.

Having arrived at the point where we encounter violence daily in our ordinary routine, we no longer expect a world without violence. Part of this is due to the governments of the world who maintain their image of power through a proliferation of violence. The results of this overabundance have great repercussions on the individual sensibility and one's relation with his environment and his fellow creatures. The movement from power to violence to the dissolution of interpersonal relationships was foreseen by Orwell when he described the philosophy of power that operated in the world of *1984:*

> The real power, the power we have to fight for night and day, is . . . power . . . over men. . . . How does one man assert his power over another . . . ? By making him suffer. Obedience is not enough. Unless he is suffering, how can you be sure that he is obeying your will and not his own? Power is in inflicting pain and humiliation. Power is in tearing human minds to pieces and putting them together again in new shapes of your own choosing. . . . A world of fear and treachery and torment, a world of trampling and being trampled upon, a world which will grow not less but *more* merciless as it refines itself. Progress in our world will be progress towards more pain . . . . We have cut the links between child and parent, and between man and man, and between man and woman. No one dares trust a wife or a child or a friend any longer. . . . If you want a picture of the future, imagine a boot stamping on a human face—forever.[10]

These words most probably no longer shock us (as they would have twenty years ago), but it is disturbing that we can read them with such sympathetic interest today because they sound so much like a sociological description of the modern abuse of power. Orwell saw clearly that violence cannot be isolated on the impersonal level of national affairs but must eventually reach down to the lowest strains in society. And violence on the highest level, the total extinction of mankind through nuclear power or by ecological imbalance, is related to alienation on the most personal level, the disillusioned individual of the 1950s and 1960s.

The basic hostility and aggressiveness of human nature has been the subject of study by artists and philosophers for many centuries. With the advent of modern psychology, man's aggressive nature came into focus through new eyes:

> . . . men are not gentle, friendly creatures wishing for love, who simply defend themselves if they are attacked . . . a powerful measure of desire for aggression has to be reckoned as part of their intrinsic instinctual endowment. The result is that their neighbor is to them not only a possible helper or sexual object, but also someone who tempts them to satisfy their aggressiveness on him, to exploit his capacity for work without his consent, to seize his possessions, to humiliate him, to cause him pain, to torture and to kill him. *Homo homini lupus.* . . .[11]

If, as Freud maintains, such an endowment is part of man's nature, why should we be distressed in our modern world when we see the working out of these aggressions? Mainly because at no other time in history has there been such a tension between the emphasis on individual liberty and identity, and the loss of meaning in life. Modern technology denies man the self-expression and freedom that history and philosophy insist are his. D. H. Lawrence fought for the liberation of man's instincts to overcome the increasing oppression brought on by an emerging industrialized society. While Lawrence's philosophy, carried to its logical end, may be terrifying, he was offering a badly needed balance to a technology that was already getting out of hand in the 1920s and 1930s. Strangely enough, in today's society Lawrence appears still more dangerous to the liberal mind: the problem of an encroaching technology has grown to such an extent that the threat of its antidote is also increased. After World War II man was left with a feeling of impotency and anonymity with which he was unable to cope. To compensate for this feeling of loss, he must assert himself in whatever way possible, the more violent and extreme the better. Instinctive action, frequently irrational and desperate, is one way of offsetting the loss of identity. Lionel Rubinoff, in *The Pornography of Power*, explains the danger of this reaction:

> . . . the real terror of anonymity lies in its potential for apocalyptic madness. For implicit in the very awareness of the powerlessness and impotency that characterizes the loss of self, and from which the self desperately seeks to escape, is an almost uncontrollable appetite for power which then expresses itself in the most violent and irrational behavior. In short, the nothingness of anonymity is filled by the pornographic pursuit of power.[12]

The abuse of power by traditional institutions within society ultimately drives the individual to assert himself by assuming his own position and weapons of power. The greater and greater impersonalization of government has strongly affected the individual's reaction, and not surprisingly he is reacting in like manner:

For the individual unable to conform to the prescriptions of his society, there is always the retreat to anarchy, delinquency and outright mutiny, while for the individual who has successfully internalized the propaganda of conformism there is the "paranoia" and violence of mass conformity, masquerading as patriotism and loyalty—as exemplified, for example, in the phenomena of racism, anti-communism, fulfilling "commitments" to "defend the freedom of less powerful nations," and crushing "riots"; phenomena which are intensified by the frustration of having been depersonalized and dehumanized.[13]

Thus, the violence that we associate with power on the higher level touches everyone and has to be reckoned with in the most personal relationships.

The poet Sylvia Plath understood this better than most writers. In a world that has gone berserk, no normal response is possible. Relationships are tainted by their environment, and what were once considered traditional qualities of love have become grotesque mockeries. In the poem "Daddy" Plath explores the world of personal relationships that are destroyed by the prevalent madness. Tenderness and affection are no longer hers, but in her need for love she opens herself to all kinds of brutality. The lover does not console and caress her, nor does the woman want such affection in a world such as this:

> Every woman adores a Fascist,
> The boot in the face, the brute
> Brute heart of a brute like you.

Violence has not replaced love in this poem but has become an integral part of it. C. B. Cox and A. R. Jones have put their critical finger on the pulse of this torturously human poem in explaining its modern historical implications:

The poem is committed to the view that this ethos of love/brutality is the dominant historical ethos of the last thirty years. The heroine carefully associates herself and her suffering with historical events. For instance, she identifies herself with the Jews and the atrocities of "Dachau, Auschwitz, Belsen" and her persecutors with Fascism and the cult of violence. The poem is more than a personal statement for by extending itself through historical images it defines the age as schizophrenic, torn between brutality and a love which in the end can only manifest itself, today, in images of violence. This love, tormented and perverse, is essentially life-denying: the only escape is into the purifying freedom of death.[14]

Death is one of the terrifying means of escape for the artist whose
sensibility is under continual attack in a deranged age. While Sylvia Plath
embraced death as a literal avenue of escape, few poets are pushed to such
extremes, for such a response endangers not only the immediate expression
of art, but indeed the survival of art itself.

The neohumanistic approach attempts to expose the unnaturalness and
dehumanizing qualities of violence while expressing strong abhorrence. The
most obvious ancestors of this kind of poetry are the trench poets of the
first World War, whose sensitivity to physical violence and its repercussions
is typified in Wilfred Owen's "Arms and the Boy":

> Let the boy try along this bayonet-blade
> How cold steel is, and keen with hunger of blood;
> Blue with all malice, like a madman's flash;
> And thinly drawn with famishing for flesh.

In "On the Death of a Murderer" John Wain examines the brutal man-
hunt for a young Nazi soldier and his murder by seemingly innocent country
people to illustrate that violence is infectious and that it has passed from
the fallen Nazis into the hands of modern civilized people. Angus Calder
muses upon the food he is eating in "Crab." His actions towards this living
creature are less than admirable: he buys the crab at the fish market, boils
it alive, and eats it in cannibalistic style. He recalls that before he immersed
it in the boiling water, he had put it on the floor "to amuse the baby."
Cruelty to a lesser form of life has a larger repercussion:

> . . . that shape which made me think
> of a soft soldier
> fried in the cockpit of a tank.

It is not difficult to recognize the humanistic and moral sentiments in this
poetry, and further discussion in chapter 5 will show this tradition is still
popular, although not conducive to the best poetry.

A somewhat newer and stranger use of violence appears in the poems
of Thom Gunn and Ted Hughes. The modern abuse of power that was
described above has moved them in a different direction from the neohumanistic poets, in such a way that they cannot simply dismiss violence as a
dehumanizing force. They have seen violence become a way of life, even
perhaps a necessary means of existence. Rather than reject such violence,
Gunn and Hughes embrace it, or at the least acknowledge it as a real and
valid form of existence at mid-century and after. They respond fully to the
call that R. D. Laing makes for a new definition of violence and love:

In the last fifty years, we human beings have slaughtered by our own hands something like seventy million of our own species. We all live under constant threat of our total annihilation. We seem to seek death and destruction as much as life and happiness. We are driven, it seems, to kill and be killed as we are to live and let live. Only by the most outrageous violation of ourselves have we achieved our capacity to live in relative adjustment to civilization, apparently driven to its own destruction. Perhaps to a limited extent we can undo what has been done to us, and what we have done to ourselves. Perhaps men and women were born to love one another, simply and genuinely, rather than to this travesty that we call love. If we can stop destroying ourselves we may stop destroying others. We have to begin by admitting and even accepting violence, rather than blindly destroying ourselves with it, and therewith we have to realize that we are as deeply afraid to live and to love as we are to die.[15]

    The first reaction to the poetry of Gunn and Hughes might be a feeling of revulsion, mainly because the twentieth-century reader has come to accept the poetic sensibility as synonymous with humane awareness and liberal responsibility. Poets who espouse "Nazi nature"[16] or "those exclusive by their action,"[17] whose marks of distinction are "the swastika-draped bed, or links that press / In twined and gleaming weight beneath a shirt"[18] do not conform to our image of the poetic temperament in an oppressive age, or in any other age.

    But the poet, because he is living in such an age, will not always find old solutions valid. The neohumanistic attitude of condemning and rejecting violence has worn thin after the poetry of World War I, the Spanish Civil War, and World War II. Philip Larkin says that he reads less and less poetry as he grows older because the poetry written by others no longer is original for him; he has already lived through the experience the poet is describing. Much of the poetry of violence will have a similar effect upon the modern reader who has in recent years nightly on the television observed American soldiers fighting in Vietnam, or Israeli planes bombing Egyptian forces along the Suez, or children starving in Biafra. To say in a poem that war and its accompanying horrors are a blight upon a civilized world will necessarily be a less effective means of communicating these horrors than seeing the dehumanizing process in action. Poetry like the following is a familiar replaying of a theme that is sounded in protest marches, television and newspaper editorials, and beer halls every week:

> Earth opens where the squandered bombs fall wide
> And all our view's a burning countryside.
> Each fairy-lamp incendiary that falls
> Is like a juggler adding to his balls,
> Tossing up more, to glitter every colour,

And when one's watched an hour, there's nothing duller.
Only the sudden metal weight of fear
Brings back the platitude that life is dear.
Keeps us awake while we sit staring out
With Reason pounding, "What's it all about?"
[Denton Welch, "Rural Raid"]

The poets who have taken it upon themselves to attack senseless violence, as in the poem above, have proved ineffective in the practical arena. The poet has never been an effective reformer of social ills, as the novelist and dramatist have proved to be at times. By their nature, the novel and drama provide more opportunity for dramatic passion and violence than the poem, and they adapt themselves more easily to contemporary social problems. One thinks back to Auden's group in the 1930s as the last poets who attempted to deal directly with the social situation. But even they became disillusioned with poetry as a reformational tool, unhappily remembering the defeat of the Republicans in the Spanish Civil War, the strength of Nazism and Fascism in Germany and Italy, the rise of the totalitarian state of the left under Stalin.

The difficulties, then, of the modern poet who must come to terms with "the pornographic pursuit of power" and its resulting violence are complex and many. The very set of social conditions that allows violence to prevail—powerful governments, an anonymous society, the threat of universal destruction—may prevent him from writing, for in comparison with these overwhelming problems, the concept of writing poetry may very well seem trivial. The poet might rant against these social conditions, but he puts himself in the vulnerable position of having his topicality limit his poetry. Sylvia Plath has said:

I do not think a "headline poetry" would interest more people any more profoundly than the headlines. And unless the up-to-the-minute poem grows out of something closer to the bone than a general, shifting philanthro and is, indeed, that unicorn-thing—a real poem, it is in danger of being screwed up as rapidly as the news sheet itself.[19]

Two problems evolve for the modern poet, both of which, I believe, are satisfactorily resolved by those poets who concern themselves with the violence of the world about them. The first is, if one must avoid topicality and at the same time wants to write what might be called involved poetry, how is he to go about it? As Robert Conquest puts it, how is the modern poet to "handle the flung world and his own heart?" The poet must absorb the cultural violence which he breathes in daily, but he must be careful not to let it appear untransformed in his poetry. A. Alvarez has described the masking process:

When I went to Auschwitz, it was the most traumatic experience I've ever been through. Even now it's still appalling. I tried to write a poem about it. I picked up the poem a couple of months later and it started changing, but it didn't come out. I recently drafted some kind of version, and completed it. There is no Auschwitz in it at all. There's nothing about the concentration camps at all. It has become a personal poem about loss.[20]

The poet in a sense serves as a sensitized filter for the violence of his world. Not that the violence is filtered out, but that in the poetic process it becomes transformed from "headline" violence to poetic violence. The method is similar for both the confessional poet and the humanistic poet. Sylvia Plath explains a similar metamorphosis of violence and abuse of power in the production of her poetry:

The issues of our time which preoccupy me at the moment are the incalculable genetic effects of fallout and a documentary article on the terrifying, mad, omnipotent marriage of big business and the military in America. ... Does this influence the kind of poetry I write? Yes, but in a sidelong fashion. I am not gifted with the tongue of Jeremiah, though I may be sleepless enough before my vision of the apocalypse. My poems do not turn out to be about Hiroshima, but about a child forming itself finger by finger in the dark. They are not about the terrors of mass extinction, but about the bleakness of the moon over a yew tree in a neighboring graveyard. Not about the testaments of tortured Algerians, but about the night thoughts of a tired surgeon.[21]

The violence that finally emerges in the poem is not necessarily recognizable as the violence of the bomb or of the streets. Frequently the poet masks the grotesque behind a veneer of civility, which the reader must first penetrate in order to understand the problem that has provoked the poet. When one reads such poetry, his first response is to accuse the poet of avoiding his traditional role of what Lionel Trilling calls "destroying the world of specious good."[22] By this he means that the modern writer

will seek to destroy . . . the habits, manners, and "values" of the bourgeois world, and not merely because these associate themselves with much that is bad, such as vulgarity, or the exploitation of the disadvantaged, but for other reasons as well, because they cloy and hamper the movement of the individual spirit toward freedom, because they prevent the attainment of "more life."[23]

It is precisely because the issues have become too great to handle in a humanistic way that the modern poet has resorted to what Hyatt Waggoner in reference to Robert Frost's poetry calls a "strategic retreat." In an age when the poet no longer has illusions of influencing the world, and the catastrophic inferences of the society in which he lives are so overwhelming that death seems a valid means of escape, it is not surprising that the post-war poet

> holds his tongue and will not spread
> More degradation in the minds of those
> Who get a pamphlet when they starve for bread.

John Press sees the problem clearly in this poem, "Unused Words," and although the poet finds himself at a loss in this society,

> he at least can try
> To learn the alphabet of truth, and spell
> The simpler intimations that it brings
> And master the technique of writing well.

This explains, in part, how the experience of Auschwitz becomes a poem of personal loss for Alvarez. It also is perhaps an explanation of the post-war poets' preoccupation with technique. As Christopher Williams has pointed out,

... what distinguishes post-war poetry from its predecessors is that its language is its main instrument of evasion. Words have ceased to act as conveyors, and instead, the language of poetry is an artificial structure. A poem is thus a game, and the sum total of its words is a private world . . . the poet is working in artificial currency.[24]

These two characteristics, the de-emphasis of important subject matter and too great concern with technique, are commonly considered the greatest handicaps of the younger poets. But we must take into consideration that they have been backed into their present posture not only in their reaction against the violence in society, but also in their reaction against the political propaganda of the 1930s and the romantic effusion of Dylan Thomas. They had learned their lesson well from Empson:

> Besides, I do not really like
> The verses about "Up the Boys,"
> The revolutionary romp,
> The hearty uproar that displays
> A sit-down literary strike. . . .
> But really does it do much good
> To put in verse however strong
> The welter of a doubt at night
> At home, in which I too belong?[25]

The question of involvement is central to the poets who are reacting against violence. How does the poet see the human race balancing somewhat perilously on the edge of extinction and not cry out in his prophetic madness? The American poets of the fifties were certainly not afraid of becoming involved with immediate problems. Ginsberg shouted, "America, go fuck yourself with your atom bomb." Rexroth, Kerouac, and other friends of the Beat Generation disengaged themselves actively from society, which was in itself an act of commitment. Or again, Ginsberg lamented at the beginning of "Howl":

> I saw the best minds of my generation destroyed by
>   madness, starving hysterical naked,
> dragging themselves through the negro streets
>   at dawn looking for an angry fix,
> angelheaded hipsters burning for the ancient
>   heavenly connection to the starry dynamo
>   in the machinery of night. . . .

His "best minds" are those who react most sensitively to the cultural forces that are most oppressive. Corso, Ginsberg, Ferlinghetti, and Burroughs attempted to disengage themselves personally from what they considered an oppressive society while their writing became less and less detached. The British poets, on the other hand, involve themselves personally in the cultural life of England (many are university teachers), while their detachment comes through the style, manner, and tone of their poetry. The frequent use of the iambic line, terza rima, and other familiar stanzaic patterns brings a respectability to their poetry which readers who most sympathize with their ideas frequently find stuffy. Sylvia Plath herself reacted to this element:

I think it [contemporary British poetry] is in a bit of a strait-jacket, if I may say so. There was an essay by Alvarez, the British critic: his arguments about the dangers of gentility in England are very pertinent, very true. I must say that I am not very genteel and I feel that gentility has a stranglehold: the neatness, the wonderful tidiness, which is so evident everywhere in England, is perhaps more dangerous than it would appear on the surface.[26]

The two volumes that heralded such gentility, *Poets of the 1950s* and *New Lines*, were accompanied by introductory statements that were originally meant to be descriptive, but were taken as prescriptive both by a somewhat hostile coterie of critics as well as by the eager young poets themselves. D. J. Enright, for example, had wanted to put together an anthology of younger poets "who steered between the rock of Wastelanditis and the whirlpool of Dylanitis."[27] Robert Conquest described the similarities of the poets in his introduction to *New Lines:* they submit "to no great systems

of theoretical constructs nor agglomerations of unconscious demands.
... On the more technical side, we see refusal to abandon a rational structure and comprehensible language, even when the verse is most highly
charged with sensuous and emotional intent."[28] While only Thom Gunn
and John Wain, of the poets under discussion in this study, were directly
connected with the Movement,[29] all except Plath have been directly affected
by the literary pronouncements about Movement poetry. The most obvious
effect is seen in their highly detached and objective style.

There have been other factors driving the poet who has been affected
by violence towards greater emotional and technical detachment. English
poetry has often been criticized for being insular, isolated from political
and literary influences beyond the boundaries of England. As recently as
1962 A. Alvarez has pleaded, with irritation, "Let us, for Christ's sake, face
the fact that we live in a pretty complicated thing called Europe and not
just a rather less complicated thing called the British Isles."[30] The literary
influences of continental Europe in the late nineteenth century were absorbed
not by English poets but by two Americans and an Irishman. Charles
Tomlinson accuses his contemporaries of neglecting Pound, Eliot, and Yeats
because they were not English. On the other hand, the retreat from engagement is defended by John Press:

> So do not blame the poet if he sings
> Of birds and flowers, or seems to concentrate
> On natural forms, as if their burgeonings
> Were all that he desired to celebrate.

Gunn and Hughes, at their best, are poets who refuse to retreat in this
manner, for they react with, not against, the violence of the world. They
are among the small number of writers who have discovered that the historical and cultural conditions during and after the war have provided a
key, not an obstacle, to greater understanding of life. The contemporary
artist, they realize, must not turn his back on or reject the power and violence to which the age has given rise, but he must in some way submit himself to these forces in order to understand them better. This is what Stephen
Spender meant when he wrote, "The greatest modern poet would be the
poet most capable of accepting the most anti-poetic and brutal phenomena
... revealing them as expressions of man's spirit even in being denials of
man's spirit."[31]

Spender, I believe, is correct. One has only to go back to volumes such
as *A Book of Verse of the Great War* and *The Poetry of War, 1939–45* to
understand what options remain open to the poet writing today. War poetry
is bloody and brutal enough, but there seldom is a submission to the violence
more often the poet sees his role as the great expositor of blood and horror

in order to illustrate the evils of war. The poetry that has resulted from the two major wars of the century has merely exhausted the possibilities for that kind of poetry. Not only does such poetry, with its built-in optimism, seem somewhat awkward and nervously out of place when read between our moods of despair and disillusionment; it is an ineffective response to the kind of violence that characterizes the postwar era:

. . . we now, for the first time, I think, in history, have not merely the means of crushing the individual as an individual but know that we have this power and are doing it scientifically. I don't think that the tortures that we inflict on one another are worse now than, say, in the Peloponnesian War, or at any time in the past; there've always been massacres and so forth, but what I think is new is the deliberate use of torture, not simply to inflict pain or to make people do what you want them to do but with the deliberate purpose of obliterating their individual identity.[32]

What response, then, is possible for the poet who will not automatically accept the traditional humanistic response? One answer is that he can embrace this violence, and however repulsive this may be to the twentieth-century sensibility, two of the best poets now writing, Thom Gunn and Ted Hughes, have chosen this course. While others bewail the loss of personal identity, these poets understand that the one way to maintain a hold on life is through violent assertion. Violence, they proclaim, is a valid way to search for meaning in the contemporary world. The presence of such a theme in their poetry is likely to bring hostile charges against them that will link them with the worst elements of the extreme right, but they have so far effectively evaded such implications.

One reason they have been able to avoid these charges is that their stand is for the most part theoretical and intellectual, not practical and active. There are exceptions to this. Both have moved to America, Hughes for long intervals, Gunn apparently on a permanent basis. The implications of such a move after the war are different from those of Auden's crossing the Atlantic earlier, for the climax of power in the United States occurred concurrently with and after World War II, while at the same time, the British Commonwealth was shrinking to that diminutive island against which the Angry Young Men so bitterly reacted. In the wake of Germany's fall the mantle of power did not descend upon Great Britain but upon the Soviet Union and the United States. We do not have to extend our imaginations very far to follow these writers, who in their poetry carry on an ideological love affair with various forms of power, in their flight from a greatly weakened country to the center of the "pursuit of power." Gunn in addition has more or less revelled in the role of a black-jacketed motorcyclist, certainly one of the most formidable symbols of power in America through the 1950s and into the 1960s. But in spite of these biographical idiosyncrasies, the main burden of their philosophy of violence is intellectual. The violence in Hughes's poetry is essentially metaphysical; and while Gunn's imagery is derived from the real world of the contorted and twisted personality, he eventually abandons that position when he sees where it is leading. In neither case can we imagine a parallel to that statement by Dali in *Diary of a Genius*, "I very much like to torture animals."

But we are still left with a nagging humanistic concern: how can we defend what ultimately becomes a philosophy of violence, the belief in violence as a valid way of life? First, it must be admitted that the neo-humanistic approach is a feeble response in our present age, precisely because it fails to understand the violence it abhors. No matter how many poems are written with the intention of instructing man that he should avoid and condemn violence, the basic conditions of human and animal nature will not disappear. The role of the artist is finally to get beyond or to transcend the violence that engulfs him. As Rubinoff suggests, "It is only when man learns how to celebrate in and ritualize his primordial disposition to evil that he can transcend it."[33] Therefore what the poet must do is not avoid the violence but indulge himself, live through it.

But how does one commit violence? Not in *fact;* for to commit it in fact is to surrender to it. To enter it through the imagination, however, is to transcend it. The existential moment is therapeutic precisely because it is imaginative. Because it is imaginative, it permits the necessary psychic distance without which there can be no transcendence. Through the imagination one can endure all manner of sin and corruption without becoming corrupt.[34]

The poet in this manner avoids the real world of violence by sublimating it in his art.

The neohumanistic poet remains detached because of his disillusionment with cosmic causes, and because of the embarrassment caused by the strident poetry of the Pylon poets and more recently that of Dylan Thomas. Although John Wain and Peter Redgrove use the language of everyday speech, they gain their detachment through an almost classical insistence on strict stanzaic patterns and traditionally metered lines. These methods are not enough to insure the hardness that perhaps they are after, but at times, as in Wain's "Cameo," this carefulness is combined with elements learned from the French symbolists to produce a sharply crystallized poem. Gunn and Hughes have no such problem achieving detachment. While the neo-humanist sees the problem of violence as essentially moral, these more reactionary poets see it as an aesthetic question. Wyndham Lewis might have been speaking for them when discussing the problem of violence in society:

Where violence is concerned, the aesthetic principle is evidently of more weight than the "moral," the latter being only the machinery to regulate the former. . . . It is along aesthetic lines that the solution of this problem should be sought rather than along moral (or police) lines, or humanitarian ones. The soberness, measure, and order that reign in all the greatest productions of art is the thing on which it is most useful to fix the mind in considering this problem. . . .[35]

Although Lewis has been harshly criticized for this approach to the problem, he is saying essentially the same thing that Rubinoff proposes: the artist has no business involving himself politically, but should experience the violence imaginatively and impose an order upon this violence through his art. Hughes himself has made a case for the poet's remaining politically uninvolved:

Damon, quoted by Plato, says that the modes of music are nowhere altered without changes in the most important laws of the state. Is a musician to listen to his gift then, or study legislation? The poet who feels he needs to mix his poetry up with significant matters, or to throw his verse into the popular excitement of the time, ought to remember this strange fact.[36]

Whether we wish to characterize the position of Hughes and Gunn as antihumanistic, antidemocratic, or simply as reactionary, historically such a stance has been marked by either aesthetic or personal withdrawal on the part of the artist. The detachment of Pound, Eliot, and Yeats in their poetry coincided with an antidemocratic approach to society. In the same pattern, it is easy to understand the need for withdrawal by those poets who after World War II see the use of power and violence as a necessary means of existence today. Among intellectuals and writers since the war, the strongest movement has been in a leftward direction. It would almost be impossible for us to imagine a contemporary poet writing the following lines about the intellectual's stand on the Vietnam War:

> Grown wiser in the company of mules
> Than they with learned pedantries of fools,
> And, since I was not sent with foreign cash,
> Like some, to spread the bolshevistic rash,
> Able both to explain the "Spanish Worker"
> From the inside, as to expound the Shirker,
> The Communist, whose bungling Left we fight
> With this Right hand—in every sense the Right![37]

An intellectual stand that is far right of center could not be displayed today with as much vigor and pride as Roy Campbell did in his poetry. For this reason these contemporary poets whose response has been in opposition to the main postwar trends have anxiously sought means to remove themselves from their poetry. Frederick Grubb, while acknowledging that "'hardness,' 'discipline' . . . a penchant for 'uniform' . . . and images of domination recur in Gunn's verse" and that "these have sinister connotations," argues that Gunn's detachment reverses their original impact. Gunn, he says, "believes in aloofness as the sine-qua-non to honest self-control."[38] Grubb, writing from a liberal point of view, attempts with great difficulty to justify the "sinister connotations" of Gunn's poetry: and he latches on to the route of escape that Gunn has conveniently provided. But this detachment is exactly the effect the poet is striving for through his aesthetic distancing, or he might find his poetry widely unacceptable to a basically liberal reading audience. Detachment does not, however, reverse a poet's assumptions any more than Yeats and Eliot can be considered less conservative in their philosophy because of their aloofness and discipline.

Both Gunn and Hughes go beyond poets like John Wain, Peter Porter, and Peter Redgrove in creating poetry of hard images and classical structures. The process of firming up their poetry goes beyond the rather simplistic technique of stanzaic patterns and measured lines, although they show themselves the masters of such forms. Broader sources of influence might be sought for their hard intellectual approach which derives from different assumptions than those of neohumanistic poetry. In spite of Charles Tomlinson's critical remark that the contemporary poet has left unexplored the territory opened by Yeats, Eliot, and Pound, it is easy to see the influence of these poets upon Gunn and Hughes. The sources may ultimately be different: Gunn says the hardness of his images derives from Donne, while denying direct influence from Eliot; and the study of Baudelaire, he claims, taught him to structure a poem. Hughes's method of freezing the dynamic into the static is similar to, if not derived from the French Symbolist method that Yeats practiced so well in his later poetry. Whether the influence of these earlier poets was conscious or not, it is obvious that their classical style was in certain ways associated with their conservative political and humanitarian stand, a fact that is also true with the more recent poets. Harrison points to this marriage of principle and style when writing of Pound:

Pound was closely associated with T. E. Hulme, Gaudier-Brzeska and Wyndham Lewis, and, to a large extent, shared their view that the coming era would be "harsh, surgical, masculine, authoritarian," bringing a reversal of the Humanist attitude in politics and philosophy, and of the Romantic attitude in the arts. This gives a real connection between fascism in politics and the neoclassic movement in the arts. . . .[39]

It is, however, too simple to parallel the classical forms of Hughes and Gunn with their reactionary themes. First, their themes are not reactionary in the traditional sense, and second, they both show an awareness of the dangerous ground on which they tread. The ambivalence towards violence that exists in their poetry produces a tension that arises from the intellectual commitment to violence and the retreat from putting such commitment into practice. This quality in Thom Gunn has made the critics John Mander and Frederick Grubb defend what appears to be his noncommittal stand before continuing to show how engaged he actually is. In certain ways the position of these two poets is similar to that of Yeats, for his attitude towards violence is heightened by the same kind of tension.

On the one hand, there is the Yeats who saw violence as a productive force in society. In "Easter 1916" the refrain "A terrible beauty is born" rings out in a tone of haunting glory. Yeats saw that even the most base could be salvaged through a kind of baptism by blood. What distinguishes this element in Yeats from the contemporary poet is that Yeats was speaking of real war and of real men being killed. Neither Gunn nor Hughes lets his poems touch on the world of the living. Even in poems such as "Elvis Presley" and "On the Move" Gunn is employing metaphor. Hughes for the most part reduces his poetry to images of the natural world and avoids the world of men. The violence that Yeats envisioned was a means of achieving a more civilized and aristocratic society, while the two contemporary poets see violence as an inescapable fact of existence in its own right. In *On the Boiler*, published in 1939, Yeats was afraid that there would be no war, and this he saw as the real danger. To him modern civilization was in a state of decay, and he thought it could only be renewed through war. He had written, " . . . love war because of the horror and because belief will be changed and civilization renewed."[40] Harrison writes of Yeats in his last years, "Total war, which was once 'bloody frivolity,' seemed to him in his last years the only way of achieving a transformation of society great enough to destroy the existing evils."[41] The immersion in violence described here is the kind that Gunn and Hughes are careful to avoid. While acknowledging the presence of violence and even the necessity of living by violence, they never try to glorify it in the same manner as Yeats. Yeats's failure is that his view of violence is ultimately corrupting, for it drives the poet himself either to indulge in this violence or to back away from his own prescriptions, which Yeats was able to do simply because he was an old man. This might make us wonder whether his relationship with Maud Gonne might have been different if Yeats had held these views earlier in his life. If Gunn and Hughes were to commit themselves to the same kind of violence that we find in the poetry of Yeats, we might also expect a greater form of participation in that violence than Gunn's motorcycling.

The more youthful Yeats, of course, would have nothing to do with violence. He was rejected by Maud Gonne in part for such timidity, and his earlier poetry was characterized by vagueness and inaction, by its mood of melancholy and romantic euphoria. In his scheme of the world permanence and stability are inherent values, and violence of any kind is a challenge to this order. The images of ferocity in Hughes's animals he would find as terrifying as the "shape with lion body and the head of a man" that foreboded evil to Yeats in the immediate future. The wild swans of Coole he sees as truer symbols of man's freedom and stability of spirit. While Gunn and Hughes both are seeking a metaphysical identity with the natural world, Yeats declares, "Once out of nature I shall never take / My bodily form from any natural thing." Yeats also believed that humanitarian ideals were responsible for violence and cruelty. There was a connection between the spread of universal education and increasing violence in society. He was not welcoming the "mere anarchy" and "the blood-dimmed tide" that was loosed upon the world. He considered violence that brought on the dissolution of society to be evil, while that which raised men to higher levels was essentially good. The tension of this stance did not exist as much within Yeats the man as within his poetry, for the attitudes outlined here represent different periods of his writing. Certain aspects seem parallel to the poetry under discussion, but to claim Yeats as an important influence upon these poets would be to stress the likenesses too strongly. The tension in the poetry of Gunn and Hughes is caused by the disparity between their intellectual stand and their approach to life, a difference that is for the modern poet a means of transcending the violence of which he writes.

And still, no other of the major twentieth-century writers seems as close to the younger poets as Yeats. Beyond this influence and similarity, close thematic parallels to their work are found in the works of the contemporary prose writers. The cultural and historical forces that influenced the artistic sensibility during and after the war were unique, and it is not difficult to see the novelists and dramatists responding to these forces in ways similar to the poets. It is no small coincidence that artists of all three genres have been attacked for producing limited and negative works. G. S. Fraser's criticism of Philip Larkin is typical of this attitude: ". . . but the strongest element [in Larkin's poetry] seems deeper, and it is an honest negative element, an accepted defeat, an insistence that a reasonable man expects rather little from life."[42] Wyndham Lewis says that this effect upon the arts is a result of the traumatic experience of living daily under the possibility of extinction: ". . . that is why talking about the alarming outlook for the fine arts appears so trivial a matter when one has finished writing about it. It is infected with the triviality of everything else."[43]

I have suggested that those who have been most touched by this triviality are those writing poetry from neohumanistic convictions. Similarly, the novelists who expose violence for the sake of denigrating its repulsive nature have not been the best novelists of the present generation. Doris Lessing is among the few who have produced first-class fiction, and one suspects her success is due to the intensity of her commitment. She, along with John Wain, has become the spokesman for the artist's responsibility to society. She has stated this philosophy: "Once a writer has a feeling of responsibility, as a human being, for the other human beings he influences, it seems to me he must become a humanist, and must feel himself as an instrument of change for good and for bad."[44] John Wain rephrases this in his terms: "The artist's function is always to *humanize* the society he is living in, to assert the importance of humanity in the teeth of whatever is currently trying to annihilate that importance."[45] Martha Quest, the heroine of Lessing's five-novel sequence *Children of Violence,* is born into and lives through an environment of ruthless and insensitive power (her Victorian parents, the South African white society, her two unsuccessful marriages, her unhappy experience with communism). In disclosing Martha's struggle to come to terms with a hostile world, Miss Lessing's intention is to "re-create warmth and humanity and love of people." George Lumley, Wain's picaresque hero of *Hurry On Down,* descends into the violent world of racketeers only to discover that life there is worse than in the respectable world of society. He accepts his niche in society as a way to rise above the problems that originally plagued him. And as one might suspect, the human-istic novel often ends in compromise. In the final scene Lumley comments on the book *Moll Flanders,* which his fiancée has been reading, "Has it got a happy ending?" Veronica, commenting on Lumley's as well as Moll's story, answers: "Not really. It doesn't end, it just stops. She turns respect-able and repents, but you knew that from the beginning."

Other novels of this type are more didactic. John Braine, in his best-seller *Room at the Top,* demonstrates that it is possible to get ahead in life through aggressiveness and ruthlessness. Joe Lampton is willing to sacrifice everything to join those who possess power; one of the persons he sacrifices is his middle-aged mistress, Alice Aisgill, whom he truly loved. Alice's death is effectively caused by Lampton himself, and Braine is care-ful that he does not escape unscathed. His worst punishment is the knowl-edge that society does not mete out justice:

"You don't see it now, but it was all for the best. She'd have ruined your whole life. Nobody blames you, love. Nobody blames you."
I pulled myself away from her abruptly.
"Oh my God," I said, "that's the trouble."

And lest the reader be fooled and think that society's failure to mete out a fitting punishment for Lampton will result in unalloyed success, Braine wrote a sequel, *Life at the Top,* that presents Joe Lampton a number of years later safely entrenched in high society and a position of power, but thoroughly wretched.

The humanistic writer is more conscious of defending his position than other writers, perhaps because his position is vulnerable under present social conditions. In an age that gives validity to various forms of power and violence, especially in the hands of institutions in suppressing the individual, no one wants to be told to be passive and yielding. John Wain, in denying the uniqueness of his age, has berated those writers who make too much of the modern condition:

> Not that anyone of my age has had to face the problems of disillusionment. About the first fact we learnt about the world we were living in was that there aren't any new starts. From the age of ten, I inhabited a world in which everyone knew that a war was coming. ... The twenties had been an enormous gate, opening on to nothing special. ... What we have to cope with is this sense of being arrested in mid-air. Our whole society is suffering from a sensation very much like the one you get if you brace yourself to jump down ten stairs and then find it was only one. And this calls into being a special kind of intellectual nuisance: the crusading modernist who is prepared to jump down ten stairs even if he has to dig a pit to do it. There he is, out of sight below ground level in his pit, but his voice can be heard continually, making the same querulous demand to the rest of us to get our spades and do some digging.[46]

He is apparently describing those who are overcome by the spirit of the times, which, in Wain's terms, is "nothing special." Those who express the hopelessness and futility of living in the present are grovelling in a pit they themselves have dug. Wain has written a novel, *Living in the Present,* that some critics have interpreted as having been written in the "pit." But the author, in his moral fashion, has defended the work: "[*Living in the Present*] was meant to be constructive, and to attack fashionable despair and nihilism." Doris Lessing has also criticized those modern writers who surrender to hopelessness: "I believe that the pleasurable luxury of despair, the acceptance of disgust, is as much a betrayal of what a writer should be as the acceptance of the simple economic view of man. ..."[48]

On the other hand, those writers "in the pit" are just as critical of moral standard-bearers. John Osborne defends the unique quality of the modern age by pointing to Eliot's relinquishing the editorship of the *Criterion* in 1939, because the times had, in Eliot's words, "induced in myself a depression of spirits so different from any other experience of fifty years as to be a new emotion." Osborne refers to the humanistic writers as "social salvage units" and is particularly direct in his attacks on John Wain and Kingsley Amis. Their kind of humanism and progress, he declares, has brought forth nothing but mass boredom and frustration, along with periodic outbreaks of world war. He also disapproves of the "adjustment" critics who oppose his plays because they present heroes who are neurotic and not like the average man. As Ian Scott-Kilvert points out, "If one takes the argument [of Osborne] one step further, the conclusion can only be that the theatre has no moral function or effect whatsoever; and that, of course, is the idea which really shocks the Adjustment Critics."[49]

Osborne's plays present characters who flail about somewhat violently but always futilely in a hopeless world. His heroes have moved beyond hope and have accepted the despair that has infected much of modern society. Archie Rice, in *The Entertainer,* is a characteristic Osborne hero driven towards despair by the modern spirit. He tries to keep alive an art of the past, vaudeville, but the sense of identity that was formerly necessary has been destroyed. Archie says, "We all had our own style, our own songs." But his father answers him, "They don't want real people any more." When the individual's identity and sense of purpose is gone, he is left with the incapacity to act. For this reason, Archie's spirit is essentially nihilistic:

I don't give a damn about anything. . . . I'm dead behind these eyes. I'm dead, just like the whole inert, shoddy lot out there. It doesn't matter because I don't feel a thing, and neither do they. We're just as dead as each other. . . . We're all just waiting for the little yellow van to come. . . .

Archie Rice is actually a further deterioration of Jimmy Porter in *Look Back in Anger,* for Jimmy at least makes an attempt at assertion through violence. But Archie has given in to the malaise of the age, and is beyond the point of reasserting himself. The refrain to his song emphasizes his philosophy: "So why, oh why should I bother to care?" Billy, his father, is from the golden age of vaudeville, when personal identity was possible and hence he was able to live more fully. Billy berates the children of the present generation with nostalgic pessimism, not with a sense of hope: "I feel sorry for you people. You don't know what it's really like. You haven't lived, most of you. You've never known what it was like, you're all miserable really. You don't know what life can be like." Archie's daughter Jean is the voice of the present who offers hope through social and moral commitment. She has taken part in a demonstration against the prime minister in Trafalgar Square, and thinks the answers to the world's problems lie in the personal sense of commitment. Osborne presents a sympathetic picture of Jean at the beginning of the play, but the strength of the "social salvage unit" comes to appear quite shoddy in contrast to Archie's open pessimism as the drama develops. Archie at one point tells her, "Listen, kiddie, you're going to find out that in the end nobody really gives a damn about anything except some little animal something."

In this last statement Archie is referring to his own sexual appetites that at least keep him moving in life, even if in no particular direction. In this respect, he moves closer to the philosophy of writers like Gunn and Hughes, who accept animal assertion as a valid response in a negative world. Archie has married twice, and his third attempt at marriage, with a twenty-year-old girl, is thwarted at the last moment by his intruding father. His entire family is aware of his sexual promiscuity, and Archie himself trades on this quality in his vaudeville routine. He informs his daughter of his sexual habits, "I'm a seven day a week man myself, twice a day." But it is clear that this kind of assertion is not sufficient to fill the need caused by Archie's loss of identity as his deterioration progresses. He prefers finally to abandon his attempts to fight back at a world intent on crushing him; he goes to jail in the end rather than accept the help of beginning a new life in Canada and thus renewing the struggle. The final stage directions emphasize Archie's insignificance and hopelessness: " . . . suddenly, the little world of light snaps out, the stage is bare and dark. Archie Rice has gone."

Samuel Beckett is another who has moved to the edges of hopelessness, and he parallels in theme what several of the poets are trying to say. His characters, like Sylvia Plath, cry out of the darkness that engulfs them. Vladimir and Estragon, in *Waiting for Godot,* are beyond the kind of negative act of which Jimmy Porter is capable. They talk of hanging themselves, but in their exhaustion they are even unable to commit this act of despair. The refrain "Nothing to be done" is repeated continually, and finally there is no longer any meaning in the act of waiting itself. Pozzo, whatever he may represent, is the most dynamic character of the play, but he is eventually debilitated through blindness, and Lucky, who in his apocalyptic speech shows a greater awareness than anyone else, is finally silenced. The ending is symbolic of Beckett's view of modern man: "Yes, let's go," says Gogo, but the stage directions are very specific: "They do not move. Curtain."

The expression of the prophets of despair is parallel to their vision of the world. *Endgame* would seem to be what its name implies, an ultimate version of deterioration. However, Beckett more recently extended these limits in a two-minute drama called *Breath,* in which the only sounds are the deep inhalation and exhalation of air and the cry of a baby; on the stage is a large heap of trash. Beckett's personal retirement from social living is a fitting complement to his terrifying vision, as Plath's suicide was the ultimate extension of her literary expression. But the limitations of both the artistic and personal expression of despair are obvious in their final forms.

There is another group of writers that see violent forces at work in society but refuse to capitulate before these forces. They express in their writings the same acceptance and acknowledgment of violence in man's nature as the poets Gunn and Hughes. On the fictional level, William Golding, Alan Sillitoe, and Anthony Powell show varying degrees of insight into this side of the human dilemma.

William Golding has taken exception to the neohumanists and the prophets of despair. He rejects their view of mankind: "I believe that man suffers from an appalling ignorance of his own nature. I produce my own view, in the belief that it may be something like the truth."[50] His novels are exceptions to the socio-realistic novels of his contemporaries, and Golding himself has characterized them as "myths." His goal is always the nature of man, and this can be examined as well under prototypical conditions as in the contemporary environment. Current affairs are merely a gauge by which to measure the basic human condition. While examining man's ferocity and brutality, he distinguishes himself from many of his contemporaries by showing this to be a universal condition, not merely the result of immediate social conditions. His first two novels, *Lord of the Flies* and *The Inheritors*, are studies in human nature, exposing the kinds of violence that man uses against his fellow man. It is understandable why these first novels have been said to comprise Golding's "primitive period."

Lord of the Flies presents a world removed from normal adult and civilized forces. The boys at first gradually and then quickly recede into a world of primordial violence. It is important to understand that Golding describes the human condition as one of aggression and hostility, in which the stronger rise up against and destroy the weaker. Piggy, the spokesman for rationality and intelligence, is ineffectual in a world governed by force and violence. Sam and Eric are the ordinary people who eventually succumb to the influence of the stronger. The boys, like modern man, are ignorant of their own nature; as Golding has said, "I think, quite simply, that they don't understand what beasts there are in the human psyche which have to be curbed."[51] The appearance of the captain of the cruiser at the end reasserts the issue of man's inclination to violence. Golding has summarized the theme as "an attempt to trace the defects of society back to the defects of human nature."[52]

While modern cultural history is not unique to Golding in revealing man's violent nature, the modern world has given a broad range of expression for this quality. In discussing how he came to write *Lord of the Flies,* Golding said that his own twentieth-century vision "had been seared by the acts of superior whites in places like Belsen and Hiroshima." The same quality in human nature is explored in *The Inheritors.* Lok and Fa are terrorized by the new people, who are more civilized but also more brutal and destructive. Modern man enters the world by crushing his immediate predecessors. Golding's aim is ultimately moral, to expose man's violent nature so that he will learn the necessity of restraint, and in this way he stands between the neohumanists and those who embrace violence. He acknowledges the violence in the world and the necessity to come to terms with it; he would not deny the place of assertiveness and aggression in human nature as the neohumanists seek to do.

Alan Sillitoe sees the violence of our present environment deriving from sociological conditions. His characters belong to the low classes and are in danger of losing what little identity they possess. Their lust for life throws them into open battle with the traditional elements of society—government, authority, middle and upper class people—and violence is a means of holding onto a world that is being destroyed. The individual feels himself the victim of technological production, impersonal war, governmental suppression. Violence, under these conditions, is a way for a person to demonstrate that he is still alive. Saul Maloff in a discussion of Sillitoe's novels has pointed to this move towards assertion:

Undoubtedly, the motive on the part of the new-left ideologists has been to give *form* as well as a historical past—to give, that is, *consciousness* to an English working class that stands in danger of losing its identity before the blandishments of (relative) affluence and debased mass culture.[53]

Sillitoe's heroes are aware that they are in a state of war. Arthur Seaton, in *Saturday Night and Sunday Morning,* comes to his vision of violence through primitive logic: those in control exist through power and violence, and the individual must counterattack by these same means. Arthur's work in the factory, his sexual promiscuity and wild drunkenness are safety valves for his explosiveness. But he realizes the extent of the war against society: ". . . there ain't much you can do about it unless you start making dynamite." When he goes for his military training, the sound and feel of his destructive power intoxicates him:

On the range he was happy with the Bren, at the thought of bullets falling into the spout from the curving magazine and at the sound of them spitting like music from the boards. He liked firing, he had to admit. It gave him satisfaction to destroy. . . . He would rather destroy something more tangible, houses or human beings, but that was impossible, yet.

Sillitoe, more than any other contemporary novelist, sees violence as a valid and necessary expression in modern culture. His heroes are similar to Gunn's in their basic anti-intellectuality and use of violence as a means to identity. Seaton, for example, feels that he is victimized by the industrial capitalists: "But if they said: 'Look, Arthur, here's a hundred weight of dynamite and a brand-new plunger, now blow up the factory,' then I'd do it, because that'd be something worth doing. Action." Gunn's heroes move "with an uncertain violence," their only direction "where the tires press." The essential difference between Sillitoe's view of the world and Gunn's and Hughes's view is the sociological element. Because Sillitoe's heroes are trying to survive in a violent world, they react violently. The origin of their actions lies in sociological sources. The condition of nature (both human and animal) that the poets describe is removed from society, and the violence that they assess is not induced by other elements in society, but originates in human nature itself. This is not to deny, of course, that the poet's own vision of violence in nature has been formed in reaction to the society in which he lives.

Anthony Powell is considered the most urbane of contemporary novelists. His long series of novels, *A Dance to the Music of Time,* revolves upon the gentle and humorous sensitivity of Nicholas Jenkins, and what Frank Kermode calls his "slow-motion people" seems far removed from violence. But through Kenneth Widmerpool, a minor yet important character who appears in all the novels as a foil to other characters, Powell makes it clear that he understands the nature of power and violence. Widmerpool during his schools days is the victim of the power of others, a latter-day Rudyard Kipling. He understands his role of victim, and from the day he is hit in the face with an overripe banana by the captain of the soccer team, he cautiously buckles under to those who are stronger. His experiences lead him eventually to reject education and learning, and gradually he forsakes his role of victim for that of victimizer. His alliance with the side of power is associated with his philistinism. The fear that haunts Jenkins is that Widmerpool is the sign of the future, a symbol of those who control the world. It is not by chance that Widmerpool's transformation from victim to victimizer occurs during World War II. One scene that gives insight into his total role occurs in *The Kindly Ones.* Jenkins and other important characters of the series are gathered at a dinner party in the castle of Sir Magnus Donners. Widmerpool appears at the castle in the middle of a game of photographing the seven deadly sins: "A man stood on the threshold. He was in uniform. He appeared to be standing at attention, a sinister, threatening figure, calling the world to arms. It was Widmerpool."

The "sinister, threatening figure" of Widmerpool in his uniform is a fitting symbol for the entire period. The sense of power and potential violence that broods over the modern world is a force with which the modern artist must reckon. For if he does not, he might be abnegating his claim to life itself. Doris Lessing has expressed this fear and hope in these words:

We are living at a time which is so dangerous, violent, explosive and precarious that it is in question whether soon there will be people left alive to

write books and to read them. It is a question of life and death for all of us;
and we are haunted, all of us, by the threat that even if some madman does
not destroy us all, our children may be born deformed or mad. We are living
at one of the great turning–points of history. In the last two decades man
has made an advance as revolutionary as when he first got off his belly and
stood upright. Yesterday, we split the atom. We assaulted that colossal cita-
del of power, the tiny unit of the substance of the universe. And because
of this, the great dream and the great nightmare of centuries of human
thought have taken flesh and walk beside us all, day and night. Artists are
the traditional interpreters of dreams and nightmares, and this is no time
to turn our backs on our traditional responsibilities, which is what we should
be doing if we refused to share in the deep anxieties, terrors and hopes of
human beings everywhere.[54]

In the following chapters then are the poets of this era who have tried to
interpret these "dreams and nightmares." And while the final judgment
may be that some have failed utterly while others have met with some success, all these artists deserve at least our attention, if not always our admiration, for their attempts to handle the "flung world" and their own hearts.

2

SYLVIA PLATH
THE INTERNALIZED RESPONSE

Sylvia Plath was not a mystic seer removed from the world about her. Of all contemporary poets, she may rightly be called the most natural child of the postwar temperament. Not only were her roots buried deep in her times, but the pressures of her involvement in contemporary culture and society finally overwhelmed her. George MacBeth has suggested that this very immediacy might be the limiting factor of her poetry:

We are too close to her work at the moment to assess clearly its final place in English literature but there is some danger that it may eventually seem too hectic and too native of the mood of the early 1960s to retain its full intensity of impact for other generations.[1]

While MacBeth recognizes that her "confessions" are native to and outgrowths of the present age, most critics have been blinded by her suicide in such a way that they can only see her poetry as the therapeutic exercises of a disturbed mind.

This psychological approach has led to the growth of what many have come to call the "myth of Sylvia Plath."[2] The final burst of energy, the predawn writing sessions, her suicide, the posthumous volumes of poetry, all gave rise to the kind of comment that Robert Lowell made in characterizing her as "one of those super-real hypnotic, great classical heroines" whose "art's immortality is life's disintegration."[3] Although it is true that her death is now inseparable from her poetry, it is better to turn to the poetry and the sources of her vision than to the effect that the modern world had upon her private life. While there appears to be a close relation between the two, we must be careful to listen more closely to the poetry than to the eerie mesmeric clamor of her death.

The violence in Sylvia Plath's poetry is very different from that in the poetry of Gunn or Hughes. She in no way welcomes violence as a means of survival in the mid-twentieth century, nor does she attempt to correct it as a perversion of man's natural state. But the world presses upon her continually, forcing her to move closer and closer to the edge of nothingness. When the choice has to be made, she chooses the final act of assertion rather than lingering dissolution in the world. Perhaps no modern poet has been more aware of the forces of power and violence in the contemporary world, and of their disintegrating effect on the individual identity. The reader of Plath's poetry must be on his guard against statements like the following that oversimplify the sense of violence in her poetry: "Sylvia Plath's posthumous collection, *Ariel*, is also filled with violence, but it is the violence of the disturbed mind rather than that of society."[4] The critic here has been snared by the myth of Sylvia Plath and as a result is unable to trace the violence to its origins. The thought of setting the poet apart from the society in which she lived, to isolate her artistic reactions within the realm of the desolate psyche, must be rejected for its narrowness, a narrowness that is repudiated by poem after poem. The violence in her poetry is a direct product of the violence in society, as the references to concentration camps, Nazi brutality and torture, wars, and suicide clearly indicate. The inner and outer worlds are brought face to face in her poetry, and the one frequently reacts to the other in chilling ways. It is this, I think, that C. B. Cox and A. R. Jones had in mind when they stated that her poetry was based on the assumption that "in a deranged world, a deranged response is the only possible reaction of the sensitive mind."[5]

The difficulty in analyzing her poetry is in coming to grips with the nature of this violence. The poet herself has been helpful in solving this problem for the thoughtful reader. In acknowledging that the issues important to her poetry were the effects of atomic fallout and the marriage of big industry with the military, she has said that these come into her poetry through very personal images: "My poems do not turn out to be about Hiroshima, but a child forming itself finger by finger in the dark."[6]

There is an element here that is both edifying and terrifying. Much of the poetry after the second World War refused to deal with problems confronting the universe. Yeats, Eliot, and Pound had carried the poetry of cosmic response to its furthest reaches in the modern world, and most poets shrank from reacting to the openly terrifying aspects of the postwar era. "Movement" poetry was low-key, emphasizing control, intelligence, and the commonplace. A. Alvarez criticized Larkin's poetry as "an attempt to show that the poet is not a strange creature inspired; on the contrary, he is just like the man next door—in fact, he probably is the man next door."[7] The reactionary tendency of this poetry finally resulted in drab, uninspiring metrical exercises that led Sylvia Plath herself to conclude that British poetry was in a "bit of a strait-jacket."[8]

Her reaction to the gentility that she found so suffocating in her British contemporaries provides a somewhat remarkable insight into the mind of the poet herself. While her poetry often astounds us, overwhelms us as it bounds along in rather reckless fashion both thematically and stylistically, she presented quite a different personal side to her friends. Nancy Hunter Steiner, her roommate at Smith College, recalls Sylvia Plath at that time, and her words surely surprised those of us who had known the poet only through her poetry:

My first impressions confirmed what seemed to be the majority opinion— that except for the penetrating intelligence and the extraordinary poetic talent she could have been an airline stewardess or the ingenuous heroine of a B movie. She did not appear tortured or alienated; at times it was difficult for me to believe that she had ever felt a self-destructive impulse. She seemed eager to create the impression of the typical American girl, the product of a hundred years of middle-class propriety. She actively disliked the little band of rebels in the house. Their bare feet, rude manners, and coarse language offended her.[9]

It is not insignificant that her poetry and public statements contradicted the image that she projected of herself. The demands of the self were different from the demands of the world, and Plath, unlike Janus, was unable to face in both directions at the same time. If she had followed either path with full commitment, she might have become, on the one hand, famous as a bohemian poet in the fifties, or, on the other, she might have abandoned poetry altogether for a more sedate, less demanding life style. Now that we see the cost of attempting to keep part of herself in each world, it is the more interesting to observe the direction of the British poets she criticized for their genteel quality.

In avoiding the horrors of the modern world, other poets were able to maintain both order and sanity. The development of Eliot and Auden perhaps warned them off. And their contemporaries in America, Ginsberg, Robert Lowell, Anne Sexton, shocked their native sense of propriety and detachment, so that many of the British poets of the 1950s and 1960s preferred to play insignificant word games rather than make themselves vulnerable to the psychological and aesthetic pitfalls that have ensnared many American poets. Sylvia Plath was able to associate with poets on both sides of the Atlantic, and while acknowledging the influence of her friend Anne Sexton and her mentor Robert Lowell, she had few nice things to say about her straitjacketed British contemporaries. In an interview on the BBC she admitted that she preferred the company of practical people to writers and artists, who "are the most narcissistic people."[10] The trouble with her poetical companions, she said, was that they "live a bit on air." While criticizing those whose poetry was detached from life, she herself intimately joined her life and her poetry. As Ted Hughes has said, "In her, as with perhaps few poets ever, the nature, the poetic genius, and the active self, were the same."[11] He further explains how the violence of her poetry was a reaction to the violence of the world:

Her reactions to hurts in other people and animals, and even tiny desecrations of plant-life were extremely violent. The chemical poisoning of nature, the pile-up of atomic waste, were horrors that persecuted her like an illness—as her latest poems record. Auschwitz and the rest were merely the open wounds, in her idea of the great civilized crime of intelligence that like the half-imbecile, omnipotent, spoiled brat Nero has turned on its mother.[12]

In the interview on the BBC referred to above, Plath said she would have liked to have been a doctor, "someone who deals directly with human experiences, is able to cure, to mend, to help, this sort of thing."[13] Her poetry, one feels, is an analogous way of dealing with a sick world. As the patient's health grew worse, the remedy (her poetry) became more intense until she was convinced that the situation was hopeless. Only then did she surrender. It is unnecessary to examine her death to understand the violence in her world; it is sufficient to read her poetry.

What we find in her poetry is a continuing examination of the violence, both physical and psychological, that surrounded her. She is unable to isolate the violence, or to objectify it in order to come to terms with it. Rather, it continually spills over into her life and even reaches into those areas that she had felt to be secure. As a result, many of her most peaceful poems seem to stand on the edge of an abyss, waiting for the calm to be violently disrupted.

This sense of violence, threatening to destroy her, demanding her soul, already is present in the very early poem "Pursuit." It is a fitting poem with which to begin a study of Plath, for the pursuit and attempted escape described here ominously portend the central thematic direction of her short poetical career. When the pursued turns to examine the pursuer, we can clearly see the poet investigating the sources of violence. Those early poems in *Colossus* were correctly seen by many reviewers as controlled and disciplined, for in many of those poems she was examining the natural habitat of violence, nature itself. When reading those earlier poems about the sow or the bull of Bendylaw, we never feel that the poet is threatened by the power that is present, although she seems fully aware of the suppressed violence in the natural world (and indeed captures that suppressed violence in a style and tone that is tensely controlled). At that point, on the contrary, there is more admiration than fear for this power which, although destructive, is not malicious.

There is a significant change in her attitude in those poems where the violence has passed from nature to man. Gone are the admiration, the idealism, the calm control. In their place we recognize a tension that can only come from fear, and the violence that she envisions in such poems as "All the Dead Dears" is ominous indeed. It is not difficult to follow the progression: the objective violence in nature could be understood, controlled, but as violence intrudes into the human world, the pressure mounts, the individual is threatened. Very soon the poems become more and more centered on the "I" who now either is drawn into or voluntarily participates in various forms of violence. As this realization grows, Plath is overcome slowly, but more and more definitely, by a paralytic impotence. Images of paralysis and stasis become increasingly obvious as she feels herself drawn more deeply into this vortex.

Such paralysis is the obvious effect of opposite forces working upon the poet's sensibility. Violent forces seduce her (or pursue her), while she is totally repelled. (The seduction/rape of Esther Greenwood in *The Bell Jar* expresses exactly this tension.) When she is able to avoid complete stasis, she vacillates between desire for and fear of commitment to life.

The struggle towards commitment is never won; her poetry becomes more despairing and she tells why she feels compelled to reject this world. She has moved beyond physical violence at this point to the examination of the psychological violence in society. Her despair grows out of the realization that the forces that could ward off the encroaching violence are absent from the world. The eventual effect is that she is faced with the loss of authority ("Little Fugue," "Lady Lazarus," "Daddy," "The Manor Garden"), the loss of love ("Elm," "The Moon and the Yew Tree," "Strumpet Song"), and ultimately the loss of identity ("Paralytic," "Strumpet Song," "In Plaster," "Suicide off Egg Rock").

In the midst of this rejection there is one positive theme that reappears in her poetry, as if she were attempting to give the world one last chance to redeem itself. For the poet, in the face of dehumanizing violence, is still desirous of committing herself to life, and so she returns to *love* as a possible means of surviving ("Blue Moles," "The Applicant," "Spinster," "Elm," "Two Views of a Cadaver Room"). With some emphasis, she determines to make a final effort, but the negative forces have taken too strong a hold; the rebirth of love is impossible. Rather than succumb passively and thus become a participant in the dehumanizing process, she advocates a final act of assertion, a final commitment to life even in the act of denying life ("Suicide off Egg Rock," "Lady Lazarus").

When Elizabeth Bishop said that because we live in a horrible and terrifying world, the worst moments of horrible and terrifying lives are an allegory of the world, she might have been referring to Sylvia Plath's poetry. Althoug Plath's earlier poems are generally considered industrious technical exercises, signs of pressure from an encroaching world of violence are already visible in the early uncollected poem "Pursuit."[14] The allegorical pursuit is by a panther that ultimately threatens her with destruction:

> There is a panther stalks me down:
> One day I'll have my death of him. ...

The animal is never identified, but it is driven towards violence and death by some primal flaw in man's nature:

> Insatiate he ransacks the land
> Condemned by our ancestral fault,
> Crying: blood, let blood be spilt.
> Meat must glut his mouth's raw wound.
> Keen the rending teeth and sweet
> The singeing fury of his fur;
> His kisses parch, each paw's a briar,
> Doom consummates that appetite.
> In the wake of this fierce cat,
> Kindled like torches for his joy,
> Charred and raven women lie,
> Become his starving body's bait.

This would be a haunting poem even if we did not have *The Bell Jar* and the later history of its author. The raw sensibility of the last poems is present, but the contrived language, the pat metaphor make it a much "safer" poem. We immediately notice her dual attitude towards the panther, the desire for and terror of surrender, an attitude that provides the tension in nearly everything she writes. The violence she faces here is both constructive and destructive: the sexual overtones are apparent and, again, this poem may have been a direct response to her first sexual experience so vividly recreated in *The Bell Jar*. There is a great deal of inhibition in her reaction to the panther, an attitude that foreshadows her feeling towards her father in later poetry. There we shall again see the distinctly sexual character of the attraction, with love and hatred blending in confused tones.

The panther invites her to participate in the world's violence through surrender to his force. What she discovers is that any act of participation, even in an attempt to fend off the pursuer, will bring on ultimate dissolution

> I hurl my heart to halt his pace,
> To quench his thirst I squander blood;
> He eats, and still his need seeks food,
> Compels a total sacrifice.

The obscure image of violence that threatened in this early poem took clear and more precise definition in later poems. The ambivalence towards these forces in life, both in animate and inanimate nature, was shaped in her earliest experiences. Her vision of the sea as a child, "the clearest thing I own,"[15] became a metaphor for her attitude towards violent forces, which she found both attractive and repulsive: "Like a deep woman, it hid a good deal; it had many faces, many delicate, terrible veils. It spoke of miracles and distances; if it could court, it could also kill."[16] Life itself, she felt, had the same qualities, but unlike Gunn and Hughes, she was unable to accommodate herself to the existence of cruelty and pain. She recalls how as a child she was appalled by violence: "But I never could watch my grandmother drop the dark green lobsters with their waving, wood-jammed claws into the boiling pot from which they would be, in a minute, drawn–red, dead, and edible. I felt the awful scald of the water too keenly on my skin."[17] The death of her father, a hurricane that wracked her grandmother's house, and the move inland all meshed together to form her final vision of childhood–"My final memory of the sea is of violence. . . ."[18]

The sensitivity to violence that she felt as a child was to have a strong impact on her mature poetic talent. Throughout her poetry there is a penetrating examination into the nature of violence, as if she hoped that deeper understanding would enable her to coexist with these forces. But although she frequently peered into what for her was the "heart of darkness," what she saw only made it more difficult for her to maintain her detachment and objectivity.

A number of her poems are descriptions of the natural world, a world in which power and violence are found in their pure state and thus are very fitting for her purposes of examination. What she sees is the domination of brute strength before which man's supposedly superior qualities are helpless. She is not content with this situation, but the lack of malice in the violence of nature enables her to accept it without great shock. "The Bull of Bendylaw" is an acknowledgment of how violence may substitute for order and reason when primitive forces are unleashed. The bull, bellowing before the sea, calls forth a violent response:

> The sea, till that day orderly,
> Hove up against Bendylaw.

The human world, the rational rule of country and animal, is left power-less before their might. The rulers either suffer paralysis of the will or be-muse themselves with ineffectual activities:

> The queen in the mulberry arbor stared
> Stiff as a queen on a playing card.
> The king fingered his beard.

The subjects are as helpless and confused as their leaders, while the more noble human attributes of kindness and intelligence are ineffective when confronted with brute force:

> The bull surged up, the bull surged down,
> Not to be stayed by a daisy chain
> Nor by any learned man.

This attitude toward the violence of nature is often close to that of Robinson Jeffers, for we feel that Sylvia Plath could accept the natural forces if man were not present. In a poem like "Sow" she shows her genu-ine admiration for "this vast Brobdingnag bulk" that still possesses its primitive instincts for sex and food. And in "Point Shirley" she exposes man's hopeless resistance to the forces of nature:

> . . . the house still hugs in each drab
> Stucco socket
> The purple egg–stones:
> . . . .
> Steadily the sea
> Eats at Point Shirley.

She continues this theme in "The Goring," a poem that seems a mixture of Hemingway and Jeffers, and shows a definite preference for the violence of the natural world to what she would consider man's *learned* violence. During a bull fight, four bulls have been killed by inept matadors in a slovenl fashion:

> The afternoon at a bad end under the crowd's truculence,
> The ritual death each time botched among dropped
>   capes, ill judged stabs.

Man's brutality is unceremonious, repellent, disgusting. The fifth bull, calling upon his primitive instincts, recaptures the dignity of violence and death:

> Instinct for art began with the bull's lofting in the mob's
> Hush a lumped man-shape. The whole act formal, fluent
>   as a dance.
> Blood faultlessly broached redeemed the sullied air,
>   the earth's grossness.

There is a clue in these last lines to Plath's art. We might naturally ask why a person of her temperament should bother to write at all; doesn't her art force her to confront the destructive forces unnecessarily? The poem is her means of bringing violence into meaningful form, as the bull's act of violence was "formal, fluent as a dance." Art, in its own way, transcends the actual and raises it to levels that reality does not encompass. It is no wonder that the poet spent such long hours on her earlier poems, carefully arranging words and rhythms in order to redeem "the sullied air, the earth's grossness." The poems of *Ariel,* however, were "rushed out at the rate of two or three a day," and the formalizing process was no longer adequate to keep art and life distinct.

The change of attitude occurs when the cycle of violence is reversed. Man, the intruder into this world of violence, is infected by these forces and turns the violence back upon the natural world. The consciousness that observes this transference sheds the mask of objective examiner more and more, and the poet becomes an open and active combatant in this struggle. No longer can she stand aside, but she is helplessly drawn into the circle of violence. In "The Rabbit Catcher" it is not just the death of the rabbit she feels, but it is the destruction of the self in her relationship with her lover:

> And we, too, had a relationship—
> Tight wires between us,
> Pegs too deep to uproot, and a mind like a ring
> Sliding shut on some quick thing,
> The constriction killing me also.

One of her best poems exploring this chain of violence is "All the Dead Dears," a meditation on the skeletons of a woman, a mouse, and a shrew that Sylvia Plath had seen in a stone coffin from the fourth century in the archaeological museum at Cambridge. The woman's anklebone had been slightly gnawed. The lesson the poet sees in this situation is that everything in nature, including man, lives off others in violence, and he who asserts himself the most vigorously shall endure the longest:

> These three, unmasked now, bear
> Dry witness

> To the gross eating game
> We'd wink at if we didn't hear
> Stars grinding, crumb by crumb,
> Our own grist down to its bony face.

Man is both victim and propagator of the "eating game" in which everyone plays a deadly role, doomed to death and birth:

> ... until we go
> Each skulled-and-crossboned Gulliver
> Riddled with ghosts, to lie
> Deadlocked with them, taking root as cradles rock.

When man competes on the level of nature, he is in danger of surrendering his humanity. This presents a particularly terrifying dilemma for the poet. If man is to retain his sensitivity and delicacy of feeling, he will perish through both the horror of his vision and the cruelty of insensitive people. M. L. Rosenthal has remarked that after reading Plath's poetry, "you would say that if a poet is sensitive enough to the age and brave enough to face it directly it will kill him through the excitation of his awareness alone."[19] The alternative is to join those insensate forces that she saw overtaking the world:

> Nudgers and shovers
> In spite of ourselves.
> Our kind multiplies:
>
> We shall by morning
> Inherit the earth.
> Our foot's in the door.
> ["Mushrooms"]

She was neither a nudger nor a shover. But her interests turned towards those who survived in that manner. As she became aware of the terrible power that could be wielded by a Hitler or a Stalin, she began reading about violent men and violent times:

I am not a historian, but I find myself reading more and more about history. I am very interested in Napoleon at the present: I'm very interested in battles in wars, in Gallipoli, the First World War and so on, and I think that as I age I am becoming more historical.[20]

However, she does not have the optimism of the young Thom Gunn, who advocates that "one joins the movement in a valueless world." Her reading of history confirms the nature of man's brutality and violence which is leading to the extinction of sensitive intelligence. "Mary's Song" is a bitter analysis of how the simplest and most innocent ideals are violated and desecrated as mankind assimilates them over the years. The virgin, singing as she watches the Christ child, contemplates how he will be attacked and murdered by those he came to help:

> The Sunday lamb cracks in its fat.

But Christ will not be the only victim, for later his death will become a holy cause for which others will be put to death. The poet sees a connection between the individual sacrifice of Christ and the institution of the church which leads to hatred and persecution of the Jews:

> The fat
> Sacrifices its opacity. . . .
>
> A window, a holy gold.
> The fire makes it precious,
> The same fire
>
> Melting the tallow heretics,
> Ousting the Jews.
> Their thick palls float
>
> Over the cicatrix of Poland, burnt-out
> Germany.

The virgin finally acknowledges that she herself participates in man's bestiality by the very fact of her humanity:

> It is a heart,
> This holocaust I walk in,
> O golden child the world will kill and eat.

The guilt by association that the poet accepts because of her participation in this imperfect humanity is central to her consciousness. She feels she is unable to escape from the dark forces of power and violence in the simplest acts of ordinary life. Situations that most of us would accept without qualms become moments of crisis and great decision for her. "The Arrival of the Bee Box" presents just such a situation. The poet's father had been an entomologist, and we know that she kept bees herself. But what would, I expect, for most people be a very ordinary experience causes great tension for Plath, exposing her fear and unwillingness to accept control over life. The box immediately takes on allegorical associations, representing the tenuous existence in which we all are locked. Except for the buzzing within, it might be mistaken for death:

> I would say it was the coffin of a midget
> Or a square baby
> Were there not such a din in it.

Locked in life, man is forced to endure this frenzy. Looking into the box, she is reminded of the blackness of Africa. In an image that recalls both Conrad and Lawrence, the poet emphasizes that commitment to life involves the release of man's dark and primitive passions, which instill fear and terror:

> It is dark, dark,
> With the swarmy feeling of African hands
> Minute and shrunk for export,
> Black on black, angrily clambering.

In anticipation of a later poem, she possibly associates the power over the bees with the terrible power she assigns to her father in "Daddy." Power there becomes identified with the worst Nazi atrocities and utter contempt for human values. Her father's work as an entomologist with the lower forms of life is analogous to the position of absolute power in which the owner of the bees finds herself. She sees herself as a god, wondering whether she should release the bees from the torment of the box: "How can I let them out?" Existence itself is the oppressor, and she is greatly disturbed that no sense can be made of this violent frenzy. As we find frequently, she can only see horror, whether she identify with the bees within, or whether she accept the responsibility as their owner. Her apparent desire is to surrender her authority over the bees. She tries to limit the situation to its actual dimensions, but she is unable to disassociate herself from the powerful rulers of the world even in her protest:

> I am not a Caesar.
> I have simply ordered a box of maniacs.
> They can be sent back.
> They can die, I can feed them nothing, I am the owner.

Her search for a way to be both committed and uncommitted exposes the dual attitude that continually bares itself in her poetry. The immediate decision is finally postponed; acting as a pleasant and agreeable god she will (at some time in the future) set them free. The box (life) is only temporary and can easily be done away with.

Her approach to life oscillates between rejection and fierce commitment, the former springing from abandoned hope, the latter, from reckless, mind-numbing desperation. Her realization of the malicious nature of violence

Paraph

drives her to attempt to change the world at one moment, but forces her into a state of depressed lethargy the next. Her environment, her exterior life, drives her forward at top speed, while she is drawn seductively towards the stasis of peace interiorly. Robert Lowell saw her caught by these forces: "She is driven forward by the pounding pistons of her heart. . . . Dangerous, more powerful than man, machine-like from hard training, she herself is a little like a racehorse, galloping relentlessly with risked, outstretched neck, deathhurdle after deathhurdle topped."[21]

There is often the hope in her poetry that total commitment to life's machinery might bring about an obliviousness to the horrors caused by that very machinery. In "Years" she rejects the "vacuous black" of eternity that elsewhere she expresses a desire of embracing:

> O God, I am not like you
> In your vacuous black, . . .
> Eternity bores me,
> I never wanted it.

She loves what repels her:

> What I love is
> The piston in motion—
> My soul dies before it.
> And the hooves of the horses,
> Their merciless churn.

The attempt at peace, stasis, in this world is impossible, and her final description of the pistons that "hiss" recalls for us subtly the myth of the garden and the snake, which in turn thematically links this poem with "Pursuit," in which poem she carefully defined the effects of "our ancestral fault."

The constant tension caused by living in a world that her sensitivity rejects gives her poetry a tone of sincerity. In "Poppies in July" the flowers are symbolic of a world that is both beautiful and dangerous:

> Little poppies, little hell flames,
> Do you do no harm?

In "Tulips" the flowers brought to her as she recovers in the hospital call her back to life, a recovery that she does not desire:

> My body is a pebble to them, they tend it as water
> Tends to the pebbles it must run over, smoothing
>   them gently.

> They bring me numbness in their bright needles, they
> bring me sleep.

The tension between the forces represented by the pistons and the tulips becomes central to nearly all the poems in *Ariel*. Perhaps if she had been able to make a choice, stasis or dynamism, sexuality or chastity, Jew or German, she might have resolved these tensions. Of if she had had a metaphysics, a larger philosophy, she might have transcended the dilemma of choice in a manner similar to Eliot's:

> At the still point of the turning world. Neither flesh
> nor fleshless;
> Neither from nor towards; at the still point,
> there the dance is,
> But neither arrest nor movement. And do not call
> it fixity,
> Where past and future are gathered. Neither
> movement from nor towards,
> Neither ascent nor decline.

It is, however, the struggle between these warring forces that makes her poetry vibrant, dramatic, and finally credible. Her poems hold the reader's attention in much the same way as dramatic narratives do except that they seldom end in pat resolutions. When she is torn in different directions, she frequently feels the compulsion to make a commitment, but too often, as in "Elm," her only act is a cry of horror:

> Now I break up in pieces that fly about like clubs.
> A wind of such violence
> Will tolerate no bystanding: I must shriek.

When we read these poems, I do not think we feel that these situations are created artificially, a manipulation of tension for the sake of art. The desire for escape is usually too intense, too impassioned, and even when there is a controlled response, as in "Gulliver," the words are dominated by a chilling sincerity. In this poem she debates whether there is a noble or dignified means of escape by rising above the trivialities and demeaning aspects of life. Gulliver, tied down by the mean and trivial, envies the clouds that float overhead:

> Over your body the clouds go
> High, high and icily . . .
> . . . .
> Unlike you,

With no strings attached.
All cool, all blue. Unlike you—
You, there on your back,
Eyes to the sky.

The tone is one of futility, of realization that he is entrapped and will never share the freedom of the clouds:

The spider-men have caught you,
Winding and twining their petty fetters,
Their bribes—
. . . .
How they hate you.

Swift and Plath were horrified by similar things in their different worlds, but she never expresses the vitriolic contempt and hatred that Swift was capable of. Even in the poem "Gulliver" he is the object of hatred, not the source. Plath is always capable of pity, frequently of disgust, never of hatred.

The futility that we sense in "Gulliver" and many other poems had its birth in various concepts: deterioration of the modern concept of authority and power, dehumanization and loss of identity, absence of love. Plath's poetry emphasizes these themes repeatedly, with a growing acknowledgment that the problems are insoluble. Her increasing sense of history must have made her aware of the modern causes for the situation, and the vision of a world informed by violence heightened the intensity of her poetry. One critic, aware of the psychological and social pressures under which she was writing, points to the relevancy of her art and its accompanying risks: ". . . an art which *does* confront our present nuclear world fully and totally must be an art on the brink of the abyss; that perhaps the creative mind exploring its innermost anguish is the only mirror art can hold up to us today."[22]

Sylvia Plath is affected strongly by the deterioration of those elements in society, whether they be ideas, institutions, or people, that have traditionally been centers of power and authority. In times of instability and personal crisis, men were able to turn to their leaders (church, government, family) for guidance and comfort. But in the contemporary world these forces too frequently seem to work in opposition to man's spirit rather than in conjunction with it. Such degenerating relationships between men and the sources of power have contributed greatly to the modern alienation.

In her essay *On Violence* Hannah Arendt is careful to distinguish between the concepts of power and violence. Power, she says, is a necessary function upon which society depends. Its validity rests upon a mutual respect by those who hold power and those subject to power. But in a society in which power is threatened, through the loss of respect by either one or both sides, men are tempted to substitute violence for their rightful authority. Violence she sees as basically a destructive force, whose only end is to foster greater violence: "The practice of violence . . . changes the world, but the most probably change is to a more violent world."[23] These distinctions are relevant to Plath's poetry, for the traditional symbol of power and authority, the father, loses his right to her respect, and quickly degenerates into a symbol of violence and brutality. The love/hatred is expressed in her desire to honor the father who has become equated with all that she dreads in the violent world. In "Little Fugue" the voice that she would love has its origin in a dark world that she must disassociate herself from:

> Such a dark funnel, my father!
> I see your voice
> Black and leafy, as in my childhood,
>
> A yew hedge of orders,
> Gothic and barbarous, pure German.
> Dead men cry from it.
> I am guilty of nothing.

Images of authority, war, and violence combine with the everyday to form her terrifying vision:

> And you, during the Great War
> In the California delicatessen
>
> Lopping the sausages!
> . . . .
> Red, mottled, like cut necks.

Her innocence is contrasted with his physical and mental deformity:

> I was seven, I knew nothing.
> The world occurred.
> You had one leg, and a Prussian mind.

In her most famous poem, "Daddy," she examines the difficulty of living in the shadow of collapsed authority, of the violence that she was both heir to and victim of. This poem rightfully deserves its high critical acclaim, for it captures perfectly her ambivalence towards activity and passivity in a violent world. The violence in her background demands an equal act of violence to rid herself of this burden. But such an act is negative, carrying with it the risk of ultimate destruction, for rejecting the violence of Nazi power which in various forms is the essence of the contemporary world in which she finds herself, she is rejecting life in its native sources (father), which she also loves. Thus she finally becomes the object of her own violence. A. Alvarez has commented on "Daddy":

What she does in this poem is, with a weird detachment, to turn the violence against herself so as to show that she can equal her oppressors with her self-inflicted oppression. And this is the strategy of the concentration camps. When suffering is there whatever you do, by inflicting it upon yourself, you achieve your identity, you set yourself free.[24]

Her dilemma is that in her freedom there is death: "Daddy, I have had to kill you." There was a time when she still hoped for the recovery of the traditional power that she would be able to respect and thus live with: "I used to pray to recover you." But the search for an ideal is fruitless. The father's authority becomes associated with modern abuses of power, and she guiltily assumes the role of victim:

> I thought every German was you.
> And the language obscene
>
> An engine, an engine
> Chuffing me off like a Jew.
> A Jew to Dachau, Auschwitz, Belsen.
> I began to talk like a Jew.
> I think I may well be a Jew.

There is no salvation in the traditional refuges of religion or love, for both functions have been assimilated in the Nazi pose. Love is not absent from the world, but it has assumed an element of brutality from the present age:

> Not God but a swastika
> So black no sky could squeak through.
> Every woman adores a Fascist,
> The boot in the face, the brute
> Brute heart of a brute like you.

After his death, she "tried to die / And get back, back, back to you." But she was unable to overcome him in that way. Only through accepting him in symbolic marriage can she do away with him:

> I made a model of you,
> A man in black with a Meinkampf look
>
> And a love of the rack and the screw.
> And I said I do, I do.

This marriage is a way of coming to terms with the violence of the age, something she could not accomplish through simple rejection. It is akin to the philosophical acceptance of Gunn and Hughes, although there are critical differences. The jaunty nursery-rhyme rhythm shows, as Peter Davison points out, that the poem was written "in dead earnest, as stays against confusion, that were at best only momentary."[25] We feel in the poem an attempt to halt the movement, as if the singsong lines could freeze the psychological moment in the form of fable or legend, which is indeed the effect. But the detachment that Gunn and Hughes are able to achieve is absent, and the final declaration, in its anger and frustration, is more a futile hope than a statement of fact:

> Daddy, daddy, you bastard, I'm through.

"Lady Lazarus" presents a similar genesis of modern violence, in which the Nazi concentration camp becomes a metaphor for the modern world. Seeing herself as a victim of violence, she identifies with the Jews whose existence is only measured as a physical object, the finished product of a violent game:

> A sort of walking miracle, my skin
> Bright as a Nazi lampshade,
> My right foot
>
> A paperweight,
> My face a featureless, fine
> Jew linen.

When vital human values have been taken away, there is only left an agglomeration of repulsive flesh and bones:

> The nose, the eye pits, the full set of teeth?
> The sour breath . . .

Reduced to object, she feels compelled to purge the accumulation of unwanted values. She feels the need to escape the situation through death:

> What a trash
> To annihilate each decade.

Death is not her enemy, for "It's easy enough to do it and stay put." What she dreads is her return to a deranged, violent world. She associates life with the Nazi doctor, who after the oppression of body and identity returns the Jews to health so that further cruelties may be worked against them:

So, so, Herr Doktor.
So, Herr Enemy.

I am your opus,
I am your valuable,
The pure gold baby

That melts to a shriek.
I turn and burn.

The return to life has then even further reduced her as an object. Life works on her as violently as the furnaces of Auschwitz:

Ash, ash—
You poke and stir.
Flesh, bone, there is nothing there—

A cake of soap,
A wedding ring,
A gold filling.

The historical allusions to her father and to the German abuse of power are significant and recurring elements in her vision of the world. In this wasteland, which she describes as her inheritance in "The Manor Garden," the life-giving elements are destroyed: "The fountains are dry and the roses over. / Incense of death." History bequeaths to her gifts of violence and vacuity:

History
Nourishes these broken flutings,
These crowns of acanthus,
And the crow settles her garments.
You inherit white heather, a bee's wing,

Two suicides, the family wolves,
Hours of blankness.

The world of violence that she finds herself heir to is like the splash in the water that Gunn uses to represent violence in *Positives,* but while Gunn sees the ripples that emanate as diminishing echoes, Plath sees the widening circle as a direct challenge to man's last refuges of identity and love.

The effect of violence that the poet dreads most is its dehumanizing quality, the transformation "from a live person into an automaton, an 'it' devoid of subjectivity."[26] Frequently she is caught between the violence that is used against her and the temptation to assert herself through violent action. The result is that state of passivity, of stasis, that she fears. "Paralytic"[27] reveals the state of one who is overcome and immobilized by hostile forces.

Physical paralysis is used to describe that psychological and emotional vacuity in which one's only desire is not to go on:

> It happens. Will it go on?–
> My mind a rock,
> No fingers to grip, no tongue,
> My god the iron lung. . . .

"In Plaster," another sickbed poem, describes the emotions of a person recovering from an accident while confined to a cast. The relationship between the cast and the victim of the accident, like that between the paralytic and the iron lung, is parallel to the poet's relationship with her world. Living in the cast, she is unable to coexist peacefully with it, as the cast attempts to overtake her, to smother her individuality:

> I shall never get out of this! There are two of me now:
> This new absolutely white person and the old yellow one,
> And the white person is certainly the superior one.

As time passes, the "relationship grew more intense," and the cast is determined to assert itself at the human's cost:

> . . . secretly she began to hope I'd die.
> Then she could cover my mouth and eyes, cover me entirely,
> And wear my painted face the way a mummy-case
> Wears the face of a pharaoh, though it's made of
>   mud and water.

The resolution is similar to that of "Paralytic": she is finally dominated completely, living dependently within the cast in a deathlike pose.

Like many other writers of this highly technological age, Sylvia Plath sees the entire industrialized movement to be in collusion and alliance with other forces that are mounting the attack upon man's individuality. The factory machines in "Night Shift" are both literal and symbolic substitutes for those in power who threaten the individual with the loss of identity. The pounding of these machines is a substitute for man's sexual drive, that impetus from within that in a Lawrentian way stakes man's claim to his share of life:

> It was not a heart, beating,
> That muted boom, that clangor
> Far off, not blood in the ears
> Drumming up any fever
>
> To impose on the evening.
> The noise came from the outside.

Man not only has accepted but has grown insensitive to these machines, so much so that they are "native, evidently, to / These stilled suburbs." The sexually creative act has been replaced by the violently sterile act of the machine:

> Hammers hoisted, wheels turning,
> Stalled, let fall their vertical
> Tonnage of metal and wood;
> Stunned the marrow.

In full acceptance, the machine is served by men in sterile white that emphasizes their lack of identity. The heavy hammer stamps out their souls.

A similar scene of an impersonal commercial society forms the background of "Suicide off Egg Rock." Both this and the previous poem derive from Auden's "To an Unknown Citizen" in tracing the violence against individuality to the mass-productive society:

> Behind him the hotdogs split and drizzled
> On the public grills, and the ochreous salt flats,
> Gas tanks, factory stacks—that landscape
> Of imperfections his bowels were part of—
> Rippled and pulsed in the glassy updraft.

The man who unlike the paralytic tries to assert his identity and retain his sensitivity against all these overpowering cultural factors is lost in a different way. Like the hot dogs, he is stretched mercilessly, as the sun exposes his helplessness: "Sun struck the water like a damnation. / No pit of shadow to crawl into. . . ." His only hold on identity is a reassertion as constant and machine-like as his attackers: "And his blood beating the old tattoo / I am, I am, I am." Even this ultimately fails, and he sees his body merely as "a machine to breathe and beat forever." There is no victory in survival, only compromise. It is a world in which the insensitive endure in the face of force and violence.

The poet is haunted by these effects of the continuing crescendo of violence, and is searching for a means of halting its destructive growth. She gradually abandons the hope that the violent world can be changed; her duty is to find a personal means of coping with the situation. It is not surprising that she seeks a solution in the terms of Yeats and Eliot:

> Is there no still place
> Turning and turning in the middle air,
> Untouched and untouchable?
>   ["Getting There"]

Unfortunately, she was equipped with neither the religion nor the mythology to convert this desire into principles or poems that would provide her with "a grace of sense . . . the resolution of life's partial horror." The need to escape from and at the same time to understand the vaulting chaos that was enveloping her influenced her to rise and write at four in the morning– "that still, blue, almost eternal hour before cockcrow, before the baby's cry, before the glassy music of the milkman, settling his bottles."[28]

Her poems were attempts to create order in a world of chaos, but they imposed a terrible burden upon her spirit. These poems stand beside the "terrible sonnets" of Hopkins and the *inferno* poetry of Eliot as records of those who have experienced the dark night of the soul, "her scourge to be her sweating self." Only for her there was no God to wrestle with, no "way up" to counter the "way down." She had, in effect, adhered to Eliot's advice strictly in her attempt to free herself from "this tormented mind tormenting yet":

> Descend lower, descend only
> Into the world of perpetual solitude, . . .
> Internal darkness, deprivation
> And destitution of all property,
> Desiccation of the world of sense,
> Evacuation of the world of fancy,
> Inoperancy of the world of spirit.
> ["Burnt Norton," ll. 139–43]

Both physically and psychologically she sought the still point that is surrounded by motion, and she found it when riding her horse Ariel. Her initial position is "stasis in darkness," but like the arrow that is motionless in flight (or Eliot's dust hovering in the sunlight), she exclaims:

> And I
> Am the arrow,
>
> The dew that flies
> Suicidal, at one with the drive
> Into the red
>
> Eye, the cauldron of morning.
> ["Ariel"]

Her desire to be in the world but not to participate in the powerful violent forces that govern the world is close to Eliot's ideal:

> The inner freedom from the practical desire,
> The release from action and suffering, release
>   from the inner
> And the outer compulsion, . . .
> ["Burnt Norton," ll. 70–73]

But Sylvia Plath never felt the release of the ecstatic moment that Eliot described ("the distraction fit, lost in a shaft of sunlight"). The still point for her was more likely to result in the involuted state of the paralytic or the insensitiveness of the mushrooms. It is perhaps her need to remain in contact with life that brings many of her poems to examine love as an answer to the dehumanizing violence that bred a Dachau and a Hiroshima.

But love quickly turns bitter to her taste, so that the poems in which she examines the elements of modern love are not traditional love poems and do not carry much hope. As in "Daddy," love itself has become infected with the brutality of the external world, so that personal relationships depend as much upon antagonism as upon tenderness for their continuance. In "Elm" the protagonist is terrified by the horrors of the day and in her despair reaches out into the night for some protection:

> I am inhabited by a cry.
> Nightly it flaps out
> Looking, with its hooks, for something to love.

In "Strumpet Song" the poet is the outsider as she sees that in modern love woman is made an object of violence by man: "Mark, I cry, that mouth / Made to do violence on." Love is no longer envisioned as a healing power, and the image of woman, reduced to sexual object, can no longer be retrieved:

> Walks there not some such one man
> As can spare breath
> To patch with brand of love this rank grimace
> Which out from black tarn, ditch and cup
> Into my most chaste own eyes
> Looks up.

The very difficulty of the syntax and rhythms of speech here reveals the tortured sensibility of the speaker. There is danger, we feel, that the chaste woman might be drawn into the world of the strumpet. Similar sexual fears are present in "Blue Moles," who in death are seen as "Blind twins bitten by bad nature." She identifies with the moles, and sees their scavenging as an analogy for the sexual act. In its constant repetition, there is no ultimate conclusion or satisfaction:

> And still the heaven
> Of final surfeit is just as far
> From the door as ever.

The act that occurs in darkness, as a stopgap against hopelessness, can never be fulfilling in a permanent manner:

> What happens between us
> Happens in darkness, vanishes
> Easy and often as each breath.

Marriage is also ineffective to revitalize the relationship between man and woman. Its effect is quite the opposite; like the society which breeds it, marriage only emphasizes the artificiality of those who would enter it:

> First, are you our sort of a person?
> Do you wear
> A glass eye, false teeth or a crutch,
> A brace or a hook,
> Rubber breasts or a rubber crotch,
>
> Stitches to show something's missing?
> ["The Applicant"]

Man has been sufficiently dehumanized so that he does not want for his marriage partner a tender, sensitive person. He would be satisfied and happier with inhuman companionship:

> Naked as paper to start
>
> But in twenty-five years she'll be silver,
> In fifty, gold.
> A living doll, everywhere you look.
> It can sew, it can cook,
> It can talk, talk, talk.

Love is similar to the inheritance of violence and vacuity in "The Manor Garden." Its most effective image is found in the first part of "Two Views of a Cadaver Room" where love, birth, and death are chillingly connected:

> In their jars the snail-nosed babies moon and glow.
> He hands her the cut-out heart like a cracked heirloom.

In the second part of the same poem, even true lovers are seen to be doomed. This section of the poem is a study of a Brueghel painting of war, in which a pair of lovers are "blind to the carrion army." Love is envisioned as a momentary protection against the violence and death of the war; but the final note is hauntingly hopeless: "These Flemish lovers flourish; not for long."

The disillusionment with love as a stabilizing force is reflected in "The Moon and the Yew Tree." The moon is a symbol of despair, whose "O-gape" has replaced the traditional values of *agape* (Christian love) and has led man into the valley of death:

The moon is no door. It is a face in its own right,
White as a knuckle and terribly upset.
It drags the sea after it like a dark crime;
    it is quiet
With the O-gape of complete despair. I live here.

With the loss of love and the onset of despair, she is deprived of the traditional comforts of religion: "The moon is my mother. She is not sweet like Mary." It is with great suffering that she gives up her simplicity and innocence that might have supported a basic faith in life. But she can no longer cling to her former beliefs, as she submits to sorrow and despair, whose symbols are the yew tree and the moon:

I have fallen a long way. Clouds are flowering
Blue and mystical over the face of the stars.
Inside the church, the saints will be all blue,
Floating on their delicate feet over the cold pews,
Their hands and faces stiff with holiness.
The moon sees nothing of this. She is bald and wild.
And the message of the yew tree is blackness—
    blackness and silence.

The poem that perhaps summarizes this response in a central symbol is "Spinster." Like the strumpet, the spinster is a product of modern love, not in her indulgence but in her rejection. She is an inhabitant of the modern wasteland, for she consciously rejects life because it lacks order and integrity ("The birds' irregular babel / And the leaves' litter / Disturb her and make her suspicious"). Life (in the poem, springtime) to her is a negative force from which she must retreat:

By this tumult afflicted, she
Observed her lover's gestures unbalance the air,
His gait stray uneven
Through a rank wilderness of fern and flower.
She judged petals in disarray,
The whole season, sloven.

The discomfort caused by the season leads her to guard against those elements that accompany the resurgence of life. She is particularly wary of the destructive male force:

And round her house she set
Such a barricade of barb and check
Against mutinous weather
As no mere insurgent man could hope to break
With curse, fist, threat
Or love, either.

The dilemma that is posed by love in "Spinster" is central to the problem as Sylvia Plath saw it in all her poetry. The creative forces of sex possess a violence that destroys one's humanity in what should be man's most positive act. The choice then is no choice, for one is destined for destruction whether he embraces love like the strumpet and the applicant or rejects love like the spinster.

All that is left is ultimate assertion: the final statement of one's humanity Life, the poet has repeated over and over, is a greater violence than death. And in death is the last great human outcry against a world that will not permit humanity to be fulfilled. This is the reason that death is so prominent a feature in Plath's life and her poetry. The man in "Suicide off Egg Rock" says with his death that he partakes in a humanity that the industrialized world behind him will not allow to exist. This is also why Lady Lazarus insists that "Dying / Is an art." Anyone can be overcome by the stronger insensitive forces and surrender his own vital forces: intellect, sensitivity, love. The art of dying is to take the violence and turn it upon oneself so that while society speaks of man's surrender before these forces, the individual knows that he has severed a diseased world from himself in asserting his full humanity:

> There would be a nobility then, there would be
>   a birthday.
> And the knife not carve, but enter
>
> Pure and clean as the cry of a baby,
> And the universe slide from my side.
>   ["A Birthday Present"]

3

THOM GUNN
THE RETREAT FROM VIOLENCE

Thom Gunn was quickly recognized as one of the most promising of the Movement poets. His tough, masculine stance coupled with a rigid classicism in his verse forms emphasized an originality that distinguished him from the other poets in *Poets of the 1950s* (1955) and *New Lines* (1956). While poets like Larkin were deliberately lowering their voices in reaction to the romantic outpourings of Dylan Thomas, Gunn chose to explore the role of the assertive will in a valueless world. His heroes were motorcyclists, historical characters noted for their insensitivity, sado-masochists. While Larkin was quietly suggesting retreat or compromise as the way to survival in the modern world, Gunn was insisting that one must impose form upon the amorphous world, and physical action, especially in some violent form, is the safest guarantee of attempting to come to terms with the world. G. S. Fraser saw Larkin as a spokesman for the middle-aged, while Gunn, he said, "is a poet who should have a peculiarly direct appeal not for angry, but for fierce young men."[1]

It is important to understand where Gunn's appeal and talent lie, for this will help to explain why this poet who was considered perhaps the best young poet of the fifties in England, "clearly England's most important export since Auden,"[2] has become a disappointment in the 1960s and 1970s.

The 1950s, especially the first half of the decade, were particularly drab years in world history. After the second World War people were willing to settle into a period of malaise, to let the struggle for power continue on international levels in cold war style except on distant fronts like Korea. In America, Eisenhower was content to set up large treaty organizations like NATO and SEATO to draw clear, definite ideological boundaries. The welfare state was in existence in England, and the English people were becoming accustomed to the idea of a reduced empire. India won its independence in 1947; the Suez Canal was nationalized by Egypt in 1956. In addition to the general feeling of compromise and retirement, the advances in technology highlighted by the orbiting of Sputnik in 1957, left the individual feeling less important in his universe. The polarization of power between the United States and the Soviet Union tended to deprive the individual of any feeling of personal power.

Against this background the poetry of Gunn amounts to a cry for the individual to reassert himself, to mold the world according to his own will instead of allowing others to create the world. Already as a student at Cambridge, Gunn recognized the danger of complacency and the necessity of avoiding it: "The danger lies in remaining in a context where values do not need to be changed, instead of keeping on the move, 'travelling light,' with less congenial associates, with less attractive surroundings, with less leisure; unknown and unsuccessful."[3] His poetry was a challenge to take on the unknown, the untried. In the struggle for identity against the background of a world that was opposed to such assertion, Gunn called upon the individual to set forth upon new territory, to release those instinctive powers that modern society had driven downwards so that they were hardly re-discoverable. The acclaim that met this early poetry was the response of an intellectual community that thirsted for a challenge to assertion, and in this sense Grubb is correct in saying that his poetry contains "the faculty of action which liberalism desperately needs."[4]

The romantic image had been driven underground in the reaction to what Enright called the "Whirlpool of Dylanitis."[5] Cascading images, uncontrollable passions, excessive emotion were consciously avoided in the poetry of the 1950s. However, Gunn's hero is basically a romantic creation, looking backwards not only to Thomas, but also to Shelley's Prometheus and Byron's Manfred. The vision of death in Thomas's "And Death Shall Have No Dominion" is not very different from Gunn's "The Unsettled Motorcyclist's Vision of His Death." All of Gunn's heroes "rage against the dying of the light."[6] But these motorcyclists, singers, dictators extend beyond the traditional romantic concept. Shelley's Promethean hero is considered a part of a liberal tradition, a movement towards community, while Gunn's protagonists, operating against the background of modern neurosis, move away from community and communication. Their actions are not other-directed, but self-directed. They assert their own humanity at the expense of the humanity of others. The search for identity, the most familiar theme in twentieth-century literature, can extend itself in either of two directions. Man can come to terms with himself in order to adjust to the world, as Lawrence's protagonists do, or he can assert himself in order to distinguish himself from the world, as Joyce's characters do. The latter is what occurs in the early poetry of Thom Gunn. What perhaps is the most terrifying element in Gunn's early poetry is the assumption on which it is founded. The poet acknowledges the violent and destructive forces at work in the world and recognizes that these forces tend to suppress and rechannel man's most basic instincts and emotions. But, rather than abhor what is occurring in society and the world at large, he admits to the validity of its existence and applies the same principles to the individual. If in the 1950s nations exist by force and violence, why not the individuals within these nations? A nation that seeks dominance in the world must make its citizens dependent on its own vision, and in this process the citizens' own instincts are lost. Their identity is linked to that of their country, and meaning comes through national victories or defeats, reminiscent of the invented wars in *1984*. Gunn sees the ultimate danger as the loss of the self in this process; the answer, however, is not retreat, compromise, or moralizing. The only viable response is to mount a struggle for survival along the same lines as the great powers do: force, violence, assertion, abuse. The search for the self is not oriented towards the world, but is egocentric, selfish, introverted, and ultimately destructive.

Although there were shocked reactions to several of these early poems that celebrate insensitive brutes, it is surprising that no one understood the full import of what Gunn was attempting. In 1963 Alan Brownjohn acknowledged "a somewhat displeasing cult of romantic toughness showing a preference at heart for the brutal, the irrational and the wilful instead of accepted humane standards."[7] More often it was considered a combination of the humane and the assertive, a marriage that was badly needed in the 1950s. But the virtue of Gunn was that he anticipated his critics. By the time Brownjohn made his criticism in 1963, the nature of Gunn's poetry had already changed. From a classical style on themes of assertion, force, and violence, his poetry became gradually freer in form and more static and meditative in theme. As the decade wore on and the tempo of violence in the world increased, Gunn seemed to realize that a quieter voice was needed. During the stagnant fifties the call to violence was necessary to shock people out of their complacency, just as Shaw's and Lawrence's call for a return to instinctive behavior was needed in earlier periods of the century. Gunn's youth was another factor in the change. All of the poems in his first volume were written while he was still a student at Cambridge, and many of them are naive in their philosophical assumptions. At that time he thought that any motion, physical or philosophical, was for its own sake valuable: "The protest resulting from disgust and uneasiness need not lead nowhere. One rejects, yes, but rejects with a purpose: by eliminating the directions already taken by the sterile, the pretentious, and the stupid, one has finally narrowed down the possibilities to one's own direction."[8] In the 1960s he rejects much of his earlier thought and admits that he was leading himself into a cul-de-sac.

Much of the fascination of Gunn's verse lies in its handling of the theme of violence. Most of the Movement poets were known for their lowered voices and simple statements; Gunn admits that the similarities among these poets were somewhat artificial, and that they were "all trying to say totally different things, and finally in different ways."[9] His success was a result of seizing on a highly relevant subject for the postwar generation, and in addressing himself to this theme he was several years ahead of his contemporaries.[10] His poetry, however, contained the seeds of its own ruin in a sense, for he left himself no room for expansion and evolution. When history overtook literature, and general violence validated what the young poet had been exploring, he had the choice of repeating himself or of branching out into new directions. After testing the first in *The Sense of Movement,* Gunn chose the latter course and took the chance of losing the support that his earlier poetry had won for him. This is in effect what happened.

When the third volume, *My Sad Captains,* appeared, there was an initial note of praise for the new direction in which the still young poet was moving. The syllabic verse and the more placid subjects were seen as a promise of mature poetic evolution, but the signs were misleading. The critics did not realize that Gunn was actually rejecting his earlier stance, and that his new poetry, carried further into still freer forms in *Positives* (1966) and *Touch* (1968), was a regression for the poet rather than an evolution. While trying to praise the last two volumes for this redirection, reviewers were unable to reconcile the later poetry with the earlier. They were relieved that Gunn had finally divorced himself from his earlier preoccupations with violence and assertion but could only praise the mellowing in general terms, unable to acknowledge a genuine improvement in his poetry. Few would agree with Patrick Swinden that the original Movement provided a base for Gunn from which he outgrew the limitations of his earlier poetry.[11] Of all the Movement poets, Gunn was the first to reach poetical maturity, but was also the first to become poetically middle-aged.

Although the poems in *Fighting Terms* showed a certain immaturity, they also promised a healthy poetic career for their young author. Many first volumes of poetry are characterized by highly personal subject matter surrounded by a pretentious technique. Gunn carved carefully wrought metaphors to carry his themes, metaphors behind which the immature poet could at times successfully hide. He was also content to let traditional meters do their work: over three-fourths of the poems are in iambic pentameter with a well-defined rhyme scheme. It is easy to praise Gunn for the mere technical expertise exhibited in this first volume, but that would detract from his real achievement of matching his classical style so consistently to his tough, desensitized, and potentially inhumane theme. When poetry is built upon images of cruelty and the domination of man by man, the poet must be careful to refrain from passionate cries for violence and abuse. Extended intricate metaphors become in such poetry more important than purely technical devices, for they are means by which the poet gains a certain detachment from distasteful or offensive subjects. The younger Gunn felt compelled to use these devices even when they were an apparent hindrance to meaning. Questioned about the difficult metaphor in "The Wound," Gunn admitted that he could easily recall the poem, but was unable to remember what idea the metaphor was intended to convey.[12] This does not sound like the same poet who wrote in a review of Empson's poetry, "The object of a poem is to say something, and, though this something may be very complicated, it is not said well by the means of irrelevant figures or a style as complicated as the subject matter."[13] One can only assume that Gunn had other reasons for employing such difficult vehicles for his ideas. It is not a matter of expressing a complicated idea with a complex metaphor, for the ideas finally prove to be quite simple. What actually occurs is that the poet gains detachment from harsh and unsympathetic themes through the use of complex metaphors. What might have otherwise been recognized and denounced as insensitive and dangerous by the poetry-reading audience was welcomed with enthusiasm. The removal of passion from his verse was Gunn's greatest assurance of acceptance.

The role of the poet in a violent world is studied in "A Mirror for Poets." The poem is a description of the Elizabethan age, but the parallel with the modern world begins with the first line: "It was a violent time." An age that is immersed in violence provides the writer not only with philosophical arguments, but with the physical material for his work:

> Wheels, racks, and fires
> In every writer's mouth, and not mere rant.

Violence presents a particular challenge to the writer whose duty it is to come to terms with his age. Gunn is of course acknowledging what he sees as his role in the modern world, and what his response should be. It is only the greatest artists who can come to grips with what is happening; "hacks" are "in the Fleet. . . . Shakespeare must keep the peace." Then in a surprising turn, the poet sets up a tension between aesthetic and physical power, as if the two sustained each other:

> ... Jonson's thumb [must]
> Be branded (for manslaughter), to the power
> Of irons the admired Southampton's power was come.

Violence is not, then, anathema in the poet's world, but an incentive to greatness, as if his writing were the spark resulting from the clash of conflicting forces. Even the queen, her "state canopied by the glamour of pain," derives benefit from the situation. Those who do not understand the nature of a violent world suffer the most, and Gunn's antidemocratic feelings are revealed at the same time:

> The faint and stumbling crowds were dim to sight
> Who had no time for pity or for terror. ...

Historians do not understand the lesson of violence, and tell us that "life meant less." Gunn rejects this. The Paphlagonian king, the original of Gloucester in *King Lear,* borrowed by Shakespeare from Sidney's *Arcadia,* could find no nobility except in a violent age. He "crouched, waiting for his greater counterpart. ... Here his huge magnanimity was born." Such an age also brings out the best in the artist, for he is forced to look at the society that thrives on violence: while Jonson was howling, "Hell's a grammar-school to this," he

> found renunciation well worth telling.
> Winnowing with his flail of comedy
> He showed coherence in society.

Again referring to his own self-proclaimed role as examiner of a violent age, the poet praises the age in which violence demands examination, refusing to let the artist ignore or reject it:

> In street, in tavern, happening would cry
> "I am myself, but part of something greater,
> Find poets what that is, do not pass by,
> For feel my fingers in your pia mater.
> I am a cruelly insistent friend:
> You cannot smile at me and make an end."

"A Mirror for Poets" is a particularly relevant poem with which to begin an examination of Gunn, for it presents many of the assumptions upon which his other poetry is built. He sees violence as a challenge to the poet, for it heightens the potential dignity and nobility of an age. Where others fail, it is the poet's role to come to terms with that violence, not through rejection, but through acceptance and understanding. In his other poetry

Gunn uses metaphors of violence to explain what is happening in the world, for violence, he would say, extends man's boundaries rather than limits them: "Here mankind might behold its whole extent."

Most of the poems in *Fighting Terms* are concerned with the problem of entering into relationships with others. They might be called love poems except that love is seen as an impossibility, and the real problem is how to maintain one's separation, not how to become united with others. Gunn's pose is established in the title of the volume, for he sees the world of personal relationships as a mirror of larger national relationships. Lovers are continually seen in the role of warriors, and the ultimate victory is subjugation of another person. The nature of love, as the poet sees it, is to take advantage of another and at all costs to maintain one's own integrity, by which he means his total isolation and independence.

The parody on Marvell's poem is obvious in the title of "To His Cynical Mistress." The woman is cynical not of his proposals but of the concept of love in today's world. Love is a great threat to their individuality, and their relation is seen as a battle. The lovers are "the two enemies" who fight not only against each other but also against the concept of love itself, embodied in Cupid, the god of love, who is "calculating," plotting to overthrow them while "promising peace." The temptation is to submit themselves to each other in love, but the lovers are "wise / To his antics" and "secretly double their spies." Their intelligence enables them to fight to a stalemate, while "on each side is the ignorant animal nation." The ignorant bodies still think that love is a joining together; but intellectually they remain suspicious while they indulge physically: "The leaders calmly plot assassination."

Gunn's objection to human relationships is based on his concept of human nature. Man asserts himself in order to maintain his individuality. In a complete relationship he would have to surrender part of his independence; in a sense he would be abandoning the search for meaning. The tension and awareness caused by interpersonal relationships can further his distinctness, as long as he does not mistake the means for the end.

The "Captain in Time of Peace" is a man who is willing to surrender his role as combatant for the security of the woman's love. He begs that she release him from his fighting posture:

> . . . what I want
> Is not the raising of a siege but this:
> Honour in the town at peace.

His tone acknowledges a loss of self-respect as he pleads, "Pity a lumpish soldier out of work. . . ." It was love that had converted him from a peaceful man to a soldier of prey:

> I was fit
> For peaceful living once, and was not born
> A clumsy brute in uniform.

When the man does not surrender himself in this fashion, when he does not surrender to the assertive role of the female, he is liable to become deranged to the opposite extreme and become the possessive lover:

> Now I will shut you in a box
> With massive sides and a lid that locks.
> ["La Prisonnière"]

Man is most contemptuous when he rejects the freedom his nature has placed upon him and thinks he can fulfill himself, like the natural world, in realizing his desires as ends:

> Only by that I can be sure
> That you are still mine and mine secure.

The narrator in this poem is far removed from the sadistic lovers who "know they shall resume pursuit, elsewhere. . . ." The lover is no lost violent soul but one of the hollow men whose damnation is his lack of action:

> But do not fear I shall keep away
> With any Miss Brown or any Miss Jones.

It is this omission of action, either positive or negative, that creates death-in-life, both for the lover and the beloved. This is the most perverse form of love:

> If my return finds a heap of bones—
> Too dry to simper, too dry to whine—
> You will still be mine and only mine.

Gunn is dissatisfied with the resolution of both these poems, for they terminate in possessive finality. If there is evil in the early poetry, it is man's sense of fulfillment. Both failure to act and completion of action are rejections of man's role. Gunn's better and most convincing poems about love study man's use of a continuing relationship as a means of deriving greater meaning from an inherently meaningless world. "Captain in Time of Peace" and "La Prisonnière" present Gunn's view of what normally occurs between man and woman: one abandons his active role by submitting to the other, which is a desecration of one's humanity. While he sees the traditional love relationship as a perversion, what society considers perversi often appears fulfilling to the poet. In "Helen's Rape" he laments the loss of primitive power in man in asserting that "Hers was the last authentic rape." Complacency and possession deaden the desire for new and strange experiences. Normal relationships work against the fullest extension of the individual, while the unusual and the difficult provide a kind of painful pleasure. Lionel Trilling aptly describes the experience which the Gunn hero is seeking:

It has always been true of some men that to pleasure they have preferred unpleasure. They imposed upon themselves difficult and painful tasks, they committed themselves to strange, "unnatural" modes of life, they sought out distressing emotions, in order to know psychic energies which are not to be summoned up in felicity. These psychic energies, even when they are experienced in self-destruction, are a means of self-definition and self-affirmation.[14]

Lofty in "Lofty in the Palais de Danse" is the embodiment of that man who chooses a momentary relationship of questionable character rather than a permanent one. His goal is to find a substitute for a woman that he once loved but who has died. The reader suspects that she was only a fanciful ideal of womanhood that has faded as he has grown older. In any case, Lofty is a scavenger who feeds upon other human beings. His interest in the girls that he picks up is purely that of a user; he is interested in neither love nor possession. Before his education to his present philosophy, Lofty was closer to the captain in the earlier poem: "I lay calm wanting nothing but what I had." His evolution to his present role is a reflection of larger events, for "like the world, I've gone to bad." As his monologue continues, he becomes a frightening figure. His world is "a deadly world: for, once I like, it kills." As a parasite, he draws the life from those he lives upon, and through destructive acts teaches others the lesson of impermanence:

> And so in me
> I kill the easy things that others like
> To teach them that no liking can be lasting.

In a world where the destructive act is accepted as normal, Lofty's response is not surprising. He mirrors the values of the world in which he lives. Platonic ideals are out of place in this environment, and Gunn's existentialism is adopted in practical style by Lofty. He does not claim that his present manner of acting is good, but assertion is his means of survival: "You praise my strength." His name ironically emphasizes the ideals from which he has fallen. Sadistic perversion replaces normal love, but Lofty points out that the girl is also an accomplice to this relationship:

> Only expected harm
> Falls from a khaki man. That's why you came
> With me and when I go you follow still.

It is significant that he wears the military khaki, for this returns him to the combative posture that Gunn stresses in relationships of this kind. Lofty cannot separate himself completely from his earlier ideals, however, and the final lines of the poem are perhaps some hint at what Gunn's later poetry would become:

> Your body is a good one, not without
> Earlier performance, but in this repeat
> The pictures are unwilled that I see bob
> Out of the dark, and you can't turn them out.

The speaker in "Carnal Knowledge" also attempts to come to terms with life through vigorous physical assertion and is fearful of losing the control of will that guarantees his identity. In the title the legal term for the sexual relationship is used in order to free the act from emotions and feeling. The poem is made more complex by the opening statement,"Even in bed I pose." Gunn's heroes in his early poetry frequently employ masks for the purpose of hiding their true feelings.[15] The lover in "Carnal Knowledge" finds the mask necessary, for the pose is his passive guard against the surrender of identity, just as his sexual activity is his active guard. His use of another person is of course a form of violence that he himself recognizes:

> I am not what I seem, believe me, so
> For the magnanimous pagan I pretend
> Substitute a forked creature as your friend.

But the sexual use of another person is, like other forms of assertion and violence, a way to survive in a hostile world, a "comical act inside the tragic game." The danger is that one might let down his guard and forget his battle stance. As soon as he realizes that she is in danger of breaking through his barrier when "in a most happy sleeping time I dreamt / We did not hold each other in contempt," he dismisses her with false arguments:

> I know of no emotion we can share.
> Your intellectual protests are a bore,
> And even now I pose, so now go. . . .

Gunn studies the evolution of his protagonist and the demise of the traditional humanistic hero in "The Court Revolt." This poem is a playing

out of Yeats's statement, "The best lack all conviction, while the worst /
Are full of passionate intensity." When man's nature releases itself in instinctive aggressiveness, the weak (Gunn would see the humanist as weak) are
crushed. They are "not overthrown by system or idea / But individual
jealousy and fear." An individual's humanity is fatal in his struggle–the
sensitive, the just, the generous are incapable of possessing and using power:

> Not that it is too much for flesh and bone
> But flesh and bone are far too much for it:
> There needs a something inhuman to fit.

The king's problem, Gunn hints, is relevant to us all. A man of great talent
is unable to use his gifts in the world: "His human flames of energy had
no place–." The human world, the only milieu in which justice, mercy,
and charity exist, has reflected these qualities:

> The grate that they were lit for would not hold,
> The vacant grates were destined to be cold.

A tension similar to that seen in several of the other poems exists here,
for Gunn seems to be struggling through a period of disillusionment. How
does one respond to the loss of humanitarian values? The man who clings
to these values is "doomed" and is caught in a crisis of paralysis:

> Not write his memoirs in America,
> Nor take a manual job with foreign men,
> Nor fight against his country, which he loved.

As if coming to terms with the problem, Gunn himself went to America
several years later. Having perhaps learned the lesson of power by that time,
he crossed the Atlantic not to escape from power but to participate very
intimately in a typically American fetish of power and violence, motorcycling.
    One feels that Gunn is ultimately trying to justify his concern for the
violent. Political causes allow men to seize power and employ violence for
seemingly valid reasons. Man submits to his primitive instincts, but hides
behind systems in finding private reasons for his public actions. In "Helen's
Rape" Gunn bemoans the loss of primitive power in its pure form. Both
men and the gods, he says, invented other stories to explain the abduction
of Helen, but the political cause is only a guise. Being afraid of his own
nature, man hides it behind noble causes. The honest man will find in violent
action an end in itself, the furthest extension of his manhood. Helen's "was
the last authentic rape" because it was accomplished for its own end.
    The violence that the poet stands most in awe of is that which seems to

have no deep or ennobling cause behind it. "Lerici" is a celebration of violence in the face of death, what would appear to be the most senseless and futile violence. Shelley he dismisses as "a minor conquest of the sea" because "he fell submissive through the waves." Gunn, like Thomas, admires those who do not go gentle into that night. Byron is more to his taste, just as the Byronic Manfred might have been the pattern for some of his poetic characters. "Byron was worth the sea's pursuit" because he would not easily submit his humanity to the sea. Vigorous, active men, like Hemingway heroes, find meaning in action itself:

> Strong swimmers, fishermen, explorers: such
> Dignify death by thriftless violence—
> Squandering all their little left to spend.

While several of the poems in this first volume, such as "Lerici" and "Helen's Rape," specifically praise violence, others show an ambiguous attitude towards the subject, as if Gunn himself were attempting to work out his ideas on the subject. The final poem, "Incident on a Journey," presents this ambiguity in dramatic terms and comes to a resolution in the refrain, "I regret nothing." He again employs the familiar metaphor of the soldier in this obvious attempt at philosophical statement. The narrator is sleeping in a cave (his own existence) when a wounded soldier appears to him in his blood-caked garments to deliver this message:

> "I am not living, in hell's pain I ache,
> *But I regret nothing.*"

Exterior reality quickly fuses with the narrator's consciousness:

> Whether his words were mine or his, in dreaming
> I found they were my deepest thought translated.

Primitive murals on the wall of the cave remind him of instinctual action that causes "no plausible nostalgia, no brown shame." In his dream the narrator-soldier relives the action that brought the soldier to his ruin, a senseless fight in a bar. The important thing was not that he had been defeated, but that he had acted from an instinctual urge:

> And always when a living impulse came
> I acted, and my action made me wise.

The message is clearly that one should live as fully as he can according to his more primitive drives without counting his gains or losses. The ambiguity

towards violent action that Gunn showed in other poems seems resolved;
he would have us believe that he has learned his lesson:

> Later I woke. I started to my feet.
> The valley light, the mist already going.
> I was alive and felt my body sweet,
> Uncaked blood in all its channels flowing.
> *I would regret nothing.*

His second volume, *The Sense of Movement* (1957), is a more satisfying
and mature volume, in which we find Gunn's best poetry. In 1954 he was
awarded a poetry scholarship to study in the United States, and since then
he has more or less adopted America as his permanent home. John Mander,
seeing *The Sense of Movement* as a direct reflection of Gunn's move to
America, views this influence on his poetry as negative.[16] However, a closer
reading of the poems in this volume will show that the effects of his move
have been mainly positive. Where he had in his earlier attempts at objectivity
and detachment retreated to unreal social contexts and difficult metaphors
so that his poems frequently became challenging riddles, the newer poems
take their metaphors from more immediate situations and their meaning
is more easily discoverable. Although choosing characters like motorcyclists
to carry his meaning leaves him open to the dangers of melodrama and
pathos, he finds in the modern tough a successful vehicle for the response
to the dilemma of modern man. The success in his choice of material gives
him greater control over subject and technique. The often stilted iambic
pentameter of *Fighting Terms* becomes more pliable without losing the
vigor that he needed to reinforce his theme. Language, theme, and form
blend in these later poems with remarkable success. With his clean and hard
language Gunn effectively filled a void in contemporary poetry to which
A. Alvarez had pointed:

What one has to do is to get a language which is tough enough, and clear
enough, and pure enough. Not tough in an Allen Ginsberg way, but in a
sort of unflinching way, in a facing what there is way, in facing what you
don't want to have to recognize. ... You create this language of the self,
and it's a language very disciplined, highly disciplined, and it's got to be
because one has not only got to write of oneself, one has also got to be
intelligent about it.[17]

With his move across the Atlantic Gunn became even more involved
with the problem of violence and with the poet's relation to this violence.
In donning his black jacket and mounting his motorcycle, he flirted with
personal immersion in the grotesque, and presumably weighed the dangers
of submerging one's aesthetic position in reality. Physical movement, he

says in "A Plan of Self-Subjection," at least provides a certain amount of protection against complacency. Writing poetry is philosophical movement, "a means of tracing circles," but at the same time it helps to impose some order upon his "fault" of reckless action. By describing actions in words, he makes the actions themselves seem exaggerated "so that my fault is worse." Added to this is the danger that poetic order will bring the contentment that his actions seek to escape; through his poetry he is afraid of "being bribed with order." He resolves that the poet's duty is to attempt to make sense out of chaos by analyzing the violent world that he inhabits. He circles "between the sky and the hot crust of hell," the order of poetry and the disorder of reality, finding both dangerous,

> Because I have found that from the heaven sun
> Can scorch like hell itself.

Salvation lies in the deliberate balance of the two:

> Here is most shade my longing, from the sun
> And that hot hell beneath.
> My circle's end is where I have begun.

He further explores the necessity for the poet to come to terms with chaotic violence in "To Yvor Winters, 1955." As some few men have control over their natural environment, the poet belongs to an elite group that creates order in its own fashion:

> Dog-generations you have trained the vigour
> That few can breed to train and fewer still
> Control with the deliberate human will.

The use of heroic couplets, a highly disciplined classical verse form, supports his point about the poet's control and order. He is tempted to relinquish his power over the cascading world of experience, "to renounce his empire over thought and speech." There is no salvation in submitting to the night of chaos; one does not give in to the darkness in a Lawrentian sense, but must come to terms with it. Such a surrender would ultimately lead to the same lack of meaning for man as exists in the universe:

> The unmotivated sadness of the air
> Filling the human with his own despair.
> Where now lies power to hold the evening back?
> Implicit in the grey is total black.

The emphasis on discovering a way to stop the flux is very close to Yeats's thought in "Byzantium," where "the smithies break the flood" through their art. The artist must exercise some control over the chaos in order to come to terms with it. Blackness is ready to erupt from "that dolphin-torn, that gong-tormented sea," unless the poet exercise both "rule and energy . . . much power in each, most in the balanced two." Rule is the classic element of control and discipline; energy, the romantic element of natural power, the assertive will:

> Ferocity existing in the fence
> Built by an exercised intelligence.

"Though night is always close," the poet must not succumb to despair but must examine life and "the force of death," while remaining "persistent, tough in will."

While some critics have seen this concern with the poet's role as a weakness, it obviously helped Gunn in his own craft. Understanding the poet's attitude towards the dilemma of chaos and order, one is able to place him more easily in historical perspective alongside Yeats, Conrad, and Lawrence. While acknowledging the creative and destructive power of the will, all three writers imposed artistic order upon chaotic movement in their attempts to understand and explain these forces. Gunn's concern with his role as artist, rather than having a negative influence, prepared him to write his best poetry on the theme of chaos and violence.

Titles are significant guides to his poetry, and one of his most important poems is "On the Move." The theme of movement for its own sake, as its own end, has been already illustrated, but here it is established in a carefully crafted philosophical statement that rests upon the contemporary metaphor of motorcyclists. As movement is a way to meaning, the more intense and violent movement becomes, the greater the guarantee that it is to contain some meaning. Man has become cut off from instinctive action, and violence is an attempt to establish contact with a more primitive and natural life. The black-jacketed motorcyclists are compared to the scuffling bluejays: the birds "follow some hidden purpose" while "the Boys . . . seek their instinct" through violent assertion of the will. By blotting out consciousness and reason, one has in truly Lawrentian fashion a chance to attain the birds' position:

> Seeking their instinct, or their poise, or both,
> One moves with an uncertain violence
> Under the dust thrown by a baffled sense
> Or the dull thunder of approximate words.

The hesitancy that is emphasized by such words as "uncertain," "baffled," "approximate" overshadows the forces of logic, reason, and temperance. The bluejay is a scavenger bird that feeds on the eggs of other birds; it survives through violence. The motorcyclists try to break through the barrier that separates them from these birds, and violent movement is an attempt to attain their instinct. The actions of the riders ally them with the animal world; from a distance they appear "as flies hanging in heat"; the noise they make is a hum (flies) that "bulges to thunder." A rejection of the intellect is implied in holding their motorcycles "by calf and thigh." They have given up their recognizable claim to humanity, hidden "in goggles, donned impersonality." Power substitutes for thought and honest examination: "they strap in doubt—by hiding it, robust." They "almost hear a meaning in their noise."

In the third stanza the poet moves beyond the earlier praise of the natural world. The birds who had appeared superior to man are now victims of his assertive will:

> They scare a flight of birds across the field:
> Much that is natural, to the will must yield.

The will, then, makes man superior, for unlike the natural creature he does not discover meaning in life but creates it as he creates himself through choice:

> Men manufacture both machine and soul,
> And use what they imperfectly control
> To dare a future from the taken routes.

Man, therefore, is not necessarily "damned because, half animal, / One lacks direct instinct." Although he is cursed with mind and thought and desire, he can find his means of escape through violent assertion, like the motorcyclists. The humanist finds it a challenge to wake "afloat on movement that divides and breaks." Through intelligence and sensitivity he tries to come to terms with the negation of values, as one sees in the poetry of Eliot, Yeats, and Auden. Instead of shoring up fragments against their ruin, Gunn's heroes respond quite differently:

> One joins the movement in a valueless world,
> Choosing it, till, both hurler and the hurled,
> One moves as well, always toward, toward.

The Boys are somewhere between bird and saint: the former has an instinctual end, the latter, a metaphysical end:

the towns they travel through
Are home for neither bird nor holiness,
For birds and saints complete their purposes.

The end of the motorcyclists is the movement itself; in moving "always
toward, toward," the repetition of the word "toward" not only emphasizes the indefinite but continued direction of the movement, but indeed,
we might read the second "toward" as an adverbial noun, as the object
of the preposition "toward." The poet concludes with a broad justification
of his activist philosophy:

At worst, one is in motion; and at best,
Reaching no absolute, in which to rest,
One is always nearer by not keeping still.

It is difficult to defend Gunn's heroes as liberals in action. In reality,
they are selfish, insensitive brutes whose reason resides in their strength. In
seeking their own identity, they would destroy the identity of others. In
"Lines for a Book" Gunn praises those who are known for their strength
and insensitivity:

I think of all the toughs through history
And thank heaven they lived, continually.

He reveals a distinct distaste for intellectuals and weaklings (he considers
them to be on the same level):

It's better
. . . .
To be a soldier than to be a cripple;
. . . .
To be insensitive, to steel the will,
Than sit irresolute all day at stool
Inside the heart. . . .

Action, not thought, is the standard by which men are valued:

I think of those exclusive by their action,
For whom mere thought could be no satisfaction.

That Gunn should choose to parody Stephen Spender's lovely poem "I
Think Continually of Those" in order to attack the sensitive, inactive man
displays a lack of both tact and feeling. When the poet's detachment breaks

down and he openly prefers his "toughs" to Spender's "truly great" who never "allow gradually the traffic to smother / With noise and fog the flowering of the spirit," the poetry itself takes on a brutish, and finally boorish, air. As he shed both mask and metaphor, Gunn was attacked harshly for his praise of insensitivity. The poet, realizing he had lowered his guard, carefully backed off from this poem, dismissing it as an insignificant poem that had little technical merit.

"The Beaters" is a further and franker extension of the theme of unnatural violent forms of love that was examined earlier in "Lofty in the Palais de Danse." Sado-masochism is a reflection of the perverse world in which the beaters live. This relationship is not so much a reaction against normal sexual behavior but a substitute for it. Nor is this for everyone, but

> Only for one who, perfect counterpart,
> Welcomes the tools of their perversity,
> Whips, cords, and strap, and toiling toward despair
> Can feel the pain sweet, tranquil, in his blood.

In warning us not to look upon the beaters too lightly, he points to the theme of violent assertion, a theme with which he showed signs of becoming dangerously preoccupied so early in his career:

> And what appear the dandy's affectation
> —The swastika-draped bed, or links that press
> In twined and gleaming weight beneath a shirt—
> Are emblems to recall identity;
> Through violent parables their special care
> Is strictly to explore that finitude.

Pain, as well as the infliction of pain, is a meaningful experience, and is a means of achieving a kind of freedom:

> Ambiguous liberty! it is the air
> Between the raised arm and the fallen thud.

Contact with another is still considered dangerous (as in "Carnal Knowledge" and the beaters avoid any permanence in these relationships. They seek no conclusion to their acts:

> It was no end, merely extremity.
> They know they shall resume pursuit, elsewhere,
> Of what they would not hold to if they could.

No answer can make them content; they shall continue pursuit in the same brutal fashion, unable to accept a meaningful relation even if their sadistic acts should lead to it. The pursuit is more important than the pursued. The only meaning that they find is that there is no meaning:

> The lips that meet the wound can finally
> Justify nothing—neither pain nor care;
> Tender upon the shoulders ripe with blood.

In advancing from the personal to the societal context, Gunn finds the city to be an appropriate parallel to the beaters. Scarred, cruel, and emptied of love, the city itself is a type of Gunn hero, "indifferent to the indifference that conceived her." A product of man's will, the city demands her own independence:

> Casual yet urgent in her love making,
> She constantly asserts her independence.

The poet does not try to see virtues in the city as Whitman and Sandburg did; he praises the city for the very thing that Eliot despised in it—its depersonalizing effect upon man. The violent man is a product of this environment:

> At the street corner, hunched up,
> he gestates action, prepared
> for some unique combat in
> boots, jeans, and a curious cap
> whose very peak, jammed forward,
> indicates resolution.

Hardened in martial discipline, "he presides in apartness, / not yet knowing his purpose / fully." His guard is not lowered "in the close / commotion of bar or bed." He waits on the street corner, ready to seek his meaning through violent action: he "fingers the blade."

Where, one must ask at this point, is the emphasis on violent action leading? The choices for Gunn were somewhat limited. On the one hand, he could have continued writing poems that glorified the philosophy of activism, but this theme had already been extended nearly as far as possible, and to pursue it further would only lead to repetition and banality. The other possibility was to move in new philosophical directions, either beyond his earlier position or in opposition to it.

In several poems there are suggestions that Gunn may have been tempted to submit to some form of traditional Christianity. In "On the Move" his envy extends to the saint as well as to the birds. And to one who is always in motion, the "self-defined," a certain peace and stability is evident in those who "complete their purposes." In "Jesus and His Mother" it may be the poet as well as Christ who is offered the shelter and safety of the garden:

> Stay in this garden ripe with pears.
> The yielding of their substance wears
> A modest and contented shine:
> And when they weep with age, not brine
> But lazy syrup are their tears.

In another poem of an obviously religious nature, "St. Martin and the Beggar," the tension between activism and religious commitment is pursued:

> "Is not this act of mine," he said,
> "A cowardly betrayal,
> Should I not peg my nature down
> With a religious nail?"

But the scarcity of poems of this nature suggests that Gunn's interest in Christian orthodoxy was a momentary diversion. Rather than pursue new, untried values, Gunn chose to reject his former stance. And while this is not fully obvious in *The Sense of Movement*, there are several poems towards the end of this volume that clearly foreshadow Gunn's poetic and philosophical adjustment.

The very title of "Legal Reform" points to this change. The poem begins with a typical Gunn metaphor for existential isolation: man is locked within the cell of self. He creates the values for himself, for "whatever it contains, my cell / Contains the absolute." But some of the hostility is gone from earlier meditations on this theme, as in "Human Condition" and "Round and Round":

> Condemned to life, a happier condemnation
> Than I deserved.

While still seeing life as a condemnation, he is more willing to make some accommodation, to live with others upon the assumption of mutual respect:

> Not till I stopped the theft of all I saw
> Just for the having's sake, could it [the new law] be passed.
> Now I refer disposal of each hour
> To this, a steady precedent at last.

While this precedent is no absolute, it is far different from only having "direction where the tires press." The stimulus for this change is the experience of a satisfactory relationship. Although he is successful in making contact outside himself, he must return at times to his cell for revitalization:

> I must get back inside the cage of breath
> For absence twitches on the loosened rope.

Exercise of his poetic powers is a satisfactory way to come to terms with life, and he hints that he is reevaluating his past experience:

> Marched off to happiness, I quarry stone
> Hour after hour, and sweat my past away.
> Already I have made, working alone,
> Notable excavations. . . .

While his poetry emphasizes the positive ("Condemned to hope, to happiness, to life,"), it has also forced him to amend his former position:

> Condemned to shift in your enclosing eyes,
> I soon correct those former notions rife
> Among the innocent, or fetter-maimed.

The last line is an obvious reference to such poems as "On the Move" and "The Beaters." Man has greater control over himself than the "manacled desire" of the Beaters would imply, "For law is in our hands, I realize." The only limitation upon man is that ultimately he is "condemned to be condemned." The ambiguity of this word, also implying that something has been proclaimed for public use, has special reference to the poet's role, for Gunn obviously is aware that through his poetry the self-centered isolation for which he had become a propagandist is doomed. His poetry does not remain a private matter, but connects him with humanity far more than the sexual pose of which he has shown himself so wary.

"The Corridor" continues the examination of the poet's role and the futility of his isolation. The corridor itself is the separation of intellect and action, the space "between the thought and felt." The protagonist is an observer of life who refuses to become involved. Squinting through a keyhole, her observes an act of love; simple observation enables him to classify the act and thus to come to terms with it: "Pleasure was simple thus; he mastered it." An old argument is then brought up: the danger lies in becoming a participant in an act that would involve the sharing of his distinctness:

> If once he acted as participant
> He would be mastered, the inhabitant
> Of someone else's world, mere shred to fit.

But this argument is refuted here, a refutation that never occurred in any earlier poem. The observer himself is being watched by the one inside; the very act of observation has become an extension of the self, a participation. For if everybody is both observer and observed, no one is independent of another. We are all involved whether we want to be or not:

> For if the watcher of the watcher shown
> There in the distant glass, should be watched too,
> Who can be master, free of others; who
> Can look around and say he is alone?

Moreover, Gunn admits that what man observes may not be the real thing, or in reference to his earlier poetry, that his vision had been distorted:

> Moreover, who can know that what he sees
> Is not distorted, that he is not seen
> Distorted by a pierglass, curved and lean?

Caught amid this uncertainty, the involved lover becomes equal to the uninvolved loner. This thought breaks the observer away from his isolated independence and urges him to an involvement with life:

> What could he do but leave the keyhole, rise,
> Holding those eyes as equal in his eyes,
> And go, one hand held out, to meet a friend?

The direction of Gunn's poetry, in response to his philosophical reevaluation, was not very clear until *My Sad Captains* appeared in 1961. This third volume breaks neatly into two parts: the first half, treating earlier themes in verse forms that characterize the first two volumes, closes off that body of his poetry which shows a preoccupation with violent action; the last half, forsaking the accustomed strict verse forms for syllabics, introduces Gunn's more static and meditative poetry.

Several poems near the beginning of *My Sad Captains* explore the poet's increasing disillusionment with his former position. The title of the volume itself refers to his fading interest in those he had previously admired: the Boys, the Beaters, Alexander, Coriolanus:

> They were men
> who, I thought, lived only to
> renew the wasteful force they
> spent with each hot convulsion.
> ["My Sad Captains"]

"In Santa Maria del Populo," one of his finest poems, is a meditation on the Caravaggio painting of Paul's conversion. The poet, undergoing a similar conversion, is attempting to understand the agony of the man lying on the ground beneath the horse:

> what is it you mean
> In that wide gesture of the lifting arms?

He turns, "hardly enlightened," to the old women praying within the church which is the home of the painting, and from this scene he understands that most men do what they can to derive some comfort from life and are not concerned with the greater metaphysical questions:

> . . . each head closeted
> In tiny fists holds comfort as it can.

The simple and limited gesture of the old women is contrasted to that wide-armed one of Paul trying to understand the world's meaning:

> Their poor arms are too tired for more than this
> —For the large gesture of solitary man,
> Resisting, by embracing, nothingness.

It is significant that Gunn emphasizes the futility of the greater gesture— the confronting of nothingness in order to ward it off. A gesture is all it is, and it is of no more success than that of the women. The assertive posture is retreating before humble acceptance.

Gunn's final break with his early position is outlined in "The Annihilation of Nothing." The abstractness and haziness that mars this poem is perhaps a reflection of his reaction against his former hardness. Forsaking the philosophy of violent assertion, he must begin once more with no assumptions:

> Nothing remained. . . .
> Stripped to indifference . . .
> I woke without desire,
> And welcomed zero as a paradigm.

His previous existential answers were a response to emptiness, but the embrace of nothingness, he seems to be saying, is not a valid response. "Nothing cannot be," and this knowledge

> Flares in the mind and leaves a smoky mark
> Of dread.
>   Look upward. Neither firm nor free,
>
> Purposeless matter hovers in the dark.

It would certainly be incorrect to accuse Gunn of establishing a teleological system, but the change from his earlier position is undeniable.

In failing to understand this metamorphosis, critics have misread other poems in the first half of this volume and have wrongly accused Gunn of an overindulgence in violence. "Black Jackets" is a parody of his own earlier themes and styles, not a further celebration of black-jacketed power. As serious poetry it could only be an inferior repetition of earlier poems. But as it slips into Hollywood clichés, the element of parody is difficult to miss:

> If it was only loss he wore,
> He wore it to assert, with fierce devotion,
>   Complicity and nothing more.
> He recollected his initiation,
>
> And one especially of the rites.
> For on his shoulders they had put tattoos:
>   The group's name on the left, The Knights,
> And on the right the slogan Born To Lose.

"Innocence" is another poem that has been improperly understood. Its effect rests upon a strong irony, for it presupposes the attitude assumed in the earlier poems. The first two stanzas are written in the earlier style and tone in praising steel-willed action and solitariness:

> He ran the course and as he ran he grew,
> And smelt his fragrance in the field. Already,
> Running he knew the most he ever knew,
> The egotism of a healthy body.

The delight with the physical is continued:

> Ran into manhood, ignorant of the past:
> Culture of guilt and guilt's vague heritage,
> Self-pity and the soul; what he possessed
> Was rich, potential, like the bud's tipped rage.

All higher qualities, conscience, feeling, soul, are removed from this man—the tone is one of praise. But as his potential becomes fully developed under the army's supervision, the tone loses its sincerity and a certain cynicism breaks through:

The Corps developed, it was plain to see,
Courage, endurance, loyalty and skill
. . . .
Hardening him to an instrument.

His innocence is like that of the motorcyclists:

A compact innocence, child-like and clear,
No doubt could penetrate, no act could harm.

Gunn stresses the ironic nature of this innocence that will suffer no questioning from within, nor any attack from without. As a purely physical person, only physical things disturb him. Seeing the Russian partisan burned alive, he feels no compunction as "the ribs wear gently through the darkening skin." He "sicken[s] only at the Northern cold," and

Could watch the fat burn with a violet flame
And feel disgusted only at the smell,
And judge that all pain finishes the same
As melting quietly by his boots it fell.

The last line, found so distasteful by many critics, captures the soldier's detachment and indifference perfectly. The violence in this poem is as grotesque as any in Gunn's poetry, but it is a necessary part of the repudiation of his former advocacy of hardness and detachment that found its conclusion in such "innocence." The poet's position at this point is not far removed from that of the humanists, discussed in chapter 5. While Gunn's poetry could not be described as moral propaganda, his poems of violence are now characterized by rejection and negation rather than by acceptance and glorification.

However, in rejecting violence as an end in itself, Gunn does not condemn violence indiscriminately. The final poem in the first section of *My Sad Captains*, "Claus von Stauffenberg," sees the bomb plot against Hitler as a valid use of violence. This action is not the assertive act for its own sake, but violence that is carefully controlled and directed by reason against other violence. The plotters are not driven by irrational forces: "Lucidity of thought draws them together." Like Brutus (whose murder of Caesar is praised), and unlike the black-jacketed boys, these men do not choose the unknown as an end in itself:

They chose the unknown . . .
. . . as a corrective.

Hitler, "whose grey eyes have filled / A nation with the illogic of their gaze," represents irrational power, while "the rational man is poised, to break, to build." The destructive act is considered positive in its larger context. Even in his failure, Claus von Stauffenberg attains a position of honor:

> And though he fails, honor personified
> In a cold time where honor cannot grow,
> He stiffens, like a statue, in mid-stride
> –Falling toward history, and under snow.

The rest of Gunn's poetry bears out his growing disillusionment with and retreat from violence. The poet himself had to come to terms with the problem of growing old and losing his physical powers. In "Modes of Pleasure" it is certainly partly himself he is describing as "the Fallen Rake, being fallen from / The heights of twenty to middle age." In the later poems of *My Sad Captains,* the violence, intensity, and brutality that had previously dominated his poetry disappear. The calming effect of the syllabic verse parallels the thematic change. Gunn explains, "When I began writing poems in syllabics a few years ago, I found that I suddenly had access to a certain spontaneity of language and perception that I hadn't been able to get when using traditional meters."[18] While the change might be welcome to the humanistic reader, and many critics greeted this turn in his poetry with unbridled joy,[19] the quality of his verse suffered. If the reader will compare a poem in the new form, such as "Light among Redwoods," with Gunn's better earlier poems, he will see that the loss of intensity is more than incidental; casualness does not rest so easily with Gunn. He has, however, taken pains to defend his syllabic verse: "I find that in syllabics I can much more easily record the casual perception, whereas with metrical verse I very often become committed to a particular kind of rather taut emotion, a rather clenched kind of emotion."[20]

The poems in the second half of *My Sad Captains,* in *Positives,* and in *Touch* display an attempt to see things as they really are rather than in the heavily metaphorical way Gunn had previously viewed them. The movement from mask to reality indicates that the poet has come to believe that the meaning behind things is not as important as the things in themselves. The quotation from Fitzgerald's *The Last Tycoon* that introduces the second part of *My Sad Captains* underlines this direction:

> I looked back as we crossed the crest of the foothills
>   –with the air so clear
> you could see the leaves on Sunset Mountains
>   two miles away.
>   It's startling to you sometimes
> –just air, unobstructed, uncomplicated air.

Objects are now valuable in themselves. In "Flying above California" he is captivated by the beauty of the land:

> Such richness can make you drunk. Sometimes
>
> on fogless days by the Pacific,
> there is a cold hard light without break
>
> that reveals merely what is—no more
> and no less.

A similar contentment with the object, freed from its symbolic connotations, is expressed in "Waking in a Newly-Built House":

> It wakes me, and my eyes rest on it,
> sharpening, and seeking merely all
> of what can be seen, the substantial,
> where the things themselves are adequate.

It is this heightened sense of observation that raises the best of these poems to a level equal to any of his earlier poems. Almost in purposeful contrast to the mindless vigor of the black-jacketed boys, the poet contemplates the slow deliberate progress of the snail:

> The snail pushes through a green
> night, for the grass is heavy
> with water and meets over
> the bright path he makes, where rain
> has darkened the earth's dark. He
> moves in a wood of desire,
>
> pale antlers barely stirring
> as he hunts. I cannot tell
> what power is at work, drenched there
> with purpose, knowing nothing.
> What is a snail's fury? All
> I think is that if later
>
> I parted the blades above
> the tunnel and saw the thin
> trail of broken white across
> litter, I would never have
> imagined the slow passion
> to that deliberate progress.

Positives, in which Gunn's verse accompanies photographs by his brother Ander Gunn, continues the mellowing of the poet. A recurring image in this volume is the rippling that emanates from a splash in the water:

> the ripples go outward
> over cool water, losing
> force ...   [p. 22]
>
> the ripples which course out from that
> centre, ridged with strength.   [p. 30]
>
> It is stone: and if ripples
> touch the base of its arches,
> he cannot feel them. ...   [p. 72]

The ripples are the energies of life that gradually dissipate as one grows older. Many of the characters in *Positives* are those who challenge life, like the younger Gunn, "inviting experience to try [them]." But as they grow older, their vision of reality changes and their smug grip on life begins to weaken. They cease the offensive that they had been waging in violent fashion, and begin to bolster their tenuous hold on the little life left to them. The hard, craggy, weatherbeaten face of an aging man shows no signs of assertion, but of retreat, or possibly of slow gradual defeat:

> The memoirs of the body
> are inscribed on it: they make
> an ambiguous story
> because you can read
> the lines two ways: as
> the ability to resist
> annihilation, or as the small
> but constant losses endured. ...   [p. 68]

Violent action with metaphysical purpose becomes less important as one approaches death. Life no longer is understood in symbolic terms, but is a reality that must be confronted on its own terms. This is the realization of the old beggar crossing the bridge:

> It is stone: and if ripples
> touch the base of its arches,
> he cannot feel them, cannot
> feel more than the flat
> stone of the bridge, and his bundle.
>
> It is not a symbolic
> bridge but a real bridge;
> nor is the bundle
> a symbol. The wind
> is cold, stone
> hard, and Salvation Army
> tea not sweet enough.   [p. 72]

In the world of harsh realities death becomes the final challenge, and it is with death that one must make his final accommodation:

> Something approaches, about
> which she has heard a good deal.
> Her deaf ears have caught it, like
> a silence in the wainscot
> by her head. Her flesh has felt
> a chill in her feet, a draught
> in her groin. She has watched it
> like moonlight on the frayed wood
> stealing toward her
> floorboard by floorboard. Will it hurt?
>
> Let it come, it is
> the terror of full repose,
> and so no terror.   [p. 78]

This volume begins with birth and ends with death while tracing the many stages in between. The youthful figures stress power and violence, like the child who derives joy from thoughts of destruction ("In a bus it is nice to ride on top because / it looks like running people over") or the young man whose animal force recalls the black-jacketed boys:

> Youth is power. He knows it,
> a rough young animal, but
> an animal that can smile.
>
> He growls playfully, shaking
> dew from the bushes
> as he pokes his way through them
> into the world beyond,
> at ease in his power. For
> can there be limits?   [p. 20]

As *Positives* traces the diminution of the ripples from the assertion of youth to the accommodation and acceptance of old age, it becomes obvious that the poet is also tracing his own development. It is surely his own poetic talent that he is evaluating in the following lines:

> Through an arc the point
> falls as force, the human
> behind it in control
> tiring, but tiring slowly . . .   [p. 52]
>
> there is a perception of
> warm water, warm, but cooling.   [p. 6]

It is not surprising, then, that a more recent volume, *Touch,* is characterized by its lack of intensity: loose thematic structure, indistinct metaphors, freer forms, colorless language. One reviewer wrote of it, "The vigor which used to give a muscular presence to his vocabulary, even when his language was that of abstraction, flags in poem after poem." One hopes that *Touch* marks the end of a period for the poet and that he will proceed to other material in future poems. The preoccupation with his role as poet and the rejection of violence have played themselves out as invigorating themes. The long poem "Misanthropos" is on one level a paradigm of the stages of Gunn's poetical development. Part 1, "The Last Man," represents the early period of existential isolation and assertive action:

> He avoids the momentous rhythm
> of the sea, one hill suffices him
> who has the entire world to choose from.
> . . . .
>   He lives like
> the birds, self-contained they hop and peck;
> . . . .
> He opens, then, a disused channel
> to the onset of hatred, until
> the final man walks the final hill
>
> without thought or feeling, as before.

In the third section of part 1, he abandons his military uniform with its hardness and discipline for the more congenial attire of nature. This new acceptance of his limitations is summarized in the fifth section:

> Bare within limits. The trick
> is to stay free within them.

In the second part, "Memoirs of the World," he rejects the abstraction and intellection that characterized his earlier work and moves towards an acceptance of the immediate in order to come to terms with death:

> . . . as I drowse I know
>
> I must keep to the world's bare surface,
> I must perceive, and perceive what is:
>
> for though the hold of perception must
> harden but diminish, like the frost,
>
> yet still there may be something retained
> against the inevitable end.

"Epitaph for Anton Schmidt" in section 11 is a repetition of the earlier poem, "Claus von Stauffenberg." He praises the German Anton Schmidt, who, in Poland, helped Jews escape from the Nazis and who was eventually executed:

> He never did mistake for bondage
> The military job, the chances,
> The limits; he did not submit
> To the blackmail of his circumstances.
> I see him in the Polish snow,
> His muddy wrappings small protection,
> Breathing the cold air of his freedom
> And treading a distinct direction.

Here is a man who breaks away from his military role to find his freedom. He is in contrast to those earlier heroes, such as Lofty and the captain in time of peace, whose martial assertion was their means to liberty.

Part 3, "Elegy on the Dust," is a lyric on the process of death and rebirth. In contemplating this cycle, the poet is struck by the sobering thought that even those who seek life through forceful action must enter death's embrace along with the most timid:

> They have all come who sought distinction hard
> To this universal knacker's yard,
> Blood dried, flesh shrivelled, and bone decimated.

Part 4, "The First Man," is a recognition of a new awareness of his own nature, and while there is a measure of the old self-confidence, there is also a sense of humility. As he tells of his rebirth into the community of man, he envisions new directions and horizons:

> His own flesh, which he hardly feels, feels dust
> Raised by the war both partly caused
> And partly fought, and yet survived. You must,
> If you can, pause; and, paused,
>
> Turn out toward others, meeting their look at full,
> Until you have completely stared
> On all there is to see. Immeasurable,
> The dust yet to be shared.

Besides this turning from the contemplation of the self to the world outside, there is a wider vision of life. The fragmentation that was seen in earlier poems has evolved into a patterned structure of life and death according to more traditional philosophies. "The Produce District" presents the decaying world of nature and man's culture:

> Now it was smell of must, rot, fungus, damp.
> The crumbling and decay accelerated,
> Old mattresses and boards in heaps
> Losing their colours with their shapes.

But against this pattern of general disintegration, which accentuates the loss of identity in a decadent society, there is regeneration even amid man's most negative acts:

> The place losing itself, lost now, unnamed,
> Birds wheeling back, with a low threshing sound.
> He aimed
> And then once more
> I heard the gun repeat
> Its accurate answer to the wilderness,
> Echoing it and making it complete.
> And maple shoots pushed upward through the ground.

The final poem in *Touch* is "Back to Life." One hopes that it is the final summing up of his earlier position, and that his return to life will eventually prove productive aesthetically as well as personally. This poem again shows a rejection of existential isolation and the violent action that resulted from that position. As he walks through the park at dusk, the street lights come on, exposing the branches of the trees as they reach out toward the light. His initial reponse is to retreat into his customary isolation, but upon reflection he sees the tree as a symbol of the life force that holds all men together. The young, "cocky with surplus strength," are self-assured in their hold on life as they walk along the curb; the old "inch down into their loosened flesh" as they sit on the benches struggling to hold onto life. The poet himself is caught between these two extremes:

> I walk between the kerb and bench
> Conscious at length
> Of sharing through each sense,
> As if the light revealed us all.
> Sustained in delicate difference
> Yet firmly growing from a single branch.

This community with mankind, both young and old, is endangered by the darkness that makes one forget the branch. He may be led to despair or he may forget the light: the branch that he grows on

> Is not remembered easily in the dark
> Or the transparency when light is gone:
> At most, a recollection

> In the mind only—over a rainswept park
> Held to by mere conviction
> In cold and misery when the clock strikes one.

The conclusion to the poem illustrates Gunn's growing preoccupation with death. It is, finally, life that prepares us, through community, for the ultimate separation:

> A small full trembling through it now
> As if each leaf were, so, better prepared
> For falling sooner or later separate.

Whether his retreat from violence will eventually have a healthy influence on Gunn's poetry is yet to be seen. His best poetry still appears in *The Sense of Movement* where he accepted the premise of violent action as a valid means of self-expression in the modern world. The loosening of language and form that accompanied this retreat accentuates the loss of vigor and intensity. Having carved his own unique place among contemporary poets in his attempts to come to terms with violence, he is in danger of becoming a "runner whom renown outran" if he is unable to free himself from the guilt and anxiety caused by his youthful acceptance of the assertive and frequently violent will.

4

TED HUGHES
ACCEPTANCE AND ACCOMMODATION

The impact of violence on the poetic sensitivity of Ted Hughes strikes a different chord than can be heard in the poetry of Sylvia Plath or Thom Gunn. Sylvia Plath was distressed by the presence of cruelty and brutality in a world that had abandoned its hold on innocence and decency; Thom Gunn examined violence as a valid means of surviving in a meaningless and cruel society, but rejected his early assertive probings in favor of a more congenial compromise. Although both of these poets initiated, in very different ways, attempts to discover means by which the sensitive and imaginative mind could accommodate itself to the particular social and historical forces of the mid–twentieth century, they express in their poetry no viable solution to the dilemma. And while solutions are not demanded of the poet in the same way that they are of a mathematician, and although asking the question might be more important than an answer, we can demand of the poet that he face the problem honestly and intelligently, and continue to struggle with those problems that he finds the most challenging. It is in this respect that Plath and Gunn are disappointing. The former in effect tells us that there is no way for the compassionate individual to exist with integrity in a society that continually wages vicious and violent attacks against his sensitivity; the latter eventually finds both the question and the attempt at answering it either too difficult or too prosaic to continue his exploration. The only contemporary British poet who has consistently explored and examined the problem of violence is Ted Hughes.

In his continuing examination of violence and its role in the world, Hughes does not choose sides for or against the forces that are set in opposition to each other, except in a few particular situations. For the most part, violence is an accepted fact of life that exists as the connecting link between all creatures in the history of the earth from prehistoric times to contemporary England, from the monsters that from "Prehistoric bedragonned times / Crawl that darkness with Latin names" to the Wodwo, who is half animal and half man, to the twentieth-century soldier in "Bayonet Charge," who listens "between his footfalls for the reason / Of his still running." Because Hughes sees the violent nature of man as a small thread in the huge tapestry of being, he has alienated those critics who apparently want him to see man's violence as unique and as an aberration of an essentially noble essence. It is also possible that in segregating his animal poetry from his human poetry, critics lose sight of the grander design. Again and again Hughes stresses the subtle connection in the primitive drives of the wind, the jaguar, the soldier, of all creation. The assertion in "Thrushes" that the artist's method is evolved from the same element that enables the animal to kill gives the lie to criticism such as Colin Falck's which accuses the poet of avoiding the real world:

... the real limitations of Hughes's animal poetry is precisely that they conjure emotions without bringing us any nearer to understanding them. They borrow their impact from a complex of emotions that they do nothing to define, and in the end tell us nothing about the urbane and civilized human world that we read the poems in.[1]

On the contrary, the animal world is used by Hughes as a means of gaining greater insights into the human world. Indeed, his concern with violence develops into a deeper investigation of its nature and source than is seen in Gunn's poetry.

Although Gunn and Hughes share elements of similarity such as their use of hard, precise images and the technique of structuring their poems in the classical tradition, there are distinctive differences that give a unique flavor to each. And after Gunn had been charged with insensitivity for his celebration of violence and power, Hughes had time to observe the dangers of taking such subjects for his poetic themes.[2]

The first accusation that the poet could expect was the cry of insensitivity, of embracing an order of brutality that was alien to humane and civilized behavior. Hughes does begin with the assumption that violence is an inherent element of all being, but this does not involve the glorification or propagation of violence through his poetry. Instead, Hughes sees that because the mainstream of twentieth-century thought, modern liberalism, has been unwilling to admit that man's nature in some way partakes of a primitive violence, man has become unable to cope with this element in his world. Like other elements of life, says Hughes, violence *in vacuo* is morally neutral and only takes on qualities of good and evil from its social and historical environment. This characteristic of not assuming a predetermined moral attitude towards the violence he details has saved Hughes from much of the harsh criticism that was aimed at Gunn. In fact, several critics have emphasized that Hughes's poems frequently express opposition to violence.[3] Daniel Hoffman goes farther in distinguishing the poetry of Hughes from earlier poetry that had come to have sinister social and political connotations: "Yet Hughes's attitude to life is by no means a celebration of its violence, as was Roy Campbell's, for, as we have seen in the war poems in his first book, Hughes register both the horror and the compassion which the inescapable violence evokes."[4]

With regard to subject matter and technique, he also shows a greater desire than Gunn to protect himself against the charges of insensitivity. The environment in which his characters are placed is less inflammatory than the motorcycle communes, the beer halls and dance halls, the beds draped with swastikas and chains that one associates with the Gunn hero. Nor does the poet himself enter into the poems as frequently; the speaker is more often a created persona than the voice of the poet. Another technique that effectively removes both reader and poet to a distance from the poem is the choice of the animal world for symbols of primitive violence and force. Ironically, by shielding himself in these ways from charges of insensitivity, Hughes opened himself up to criticism from another source. His detachment has been interpreted as a rejection of compassion and involvement with human affairs: "With Hughes the victory goes simply and completely to the images, and the result is a cruel absence of compassion and a profound denial of the capacity for growth, love, and uniqueness which makes human beings human (and not simply one more species of animal)."[5] Reacting in a similar manner Vernon Scannell has satirized Hughes's preoccupation with the animal world. Observing a cow, Scannell concludes that

> It is the anthropomorphic fallacy
> Which puts brown speculation in those eyes,
> But I am taken in . . .
> Almost, it seems, she might be contemplating
> Composing a long poem about Ted Hughes.
> ["Ruminant"]

Such criticism ultimately falls short of coming to terms with the poetry. The elements that Hughes employs to gain detachment were used by Donne and Milton, by Eliot and Yeats. Detachment implies neither insensitivity nor disengagement. Instead of seeing his nature poems as an escape from contemporary issues, critics would be better advised to take the lead from Rosenthal in seeing these poems as the product of a poetic soul formed in the crucible of recent history; Hughes's violent poetry, he says, "would have been less likely to appear before the last war. Its bloodymindedness is a reflex of recent history, the experience of the Blitz, the Bomb, and Auschwitz—an expression of them, a recoiling from them, an approach to experience by way of their implications."[6]

While Hughes is no more philosophical than Gunn, his continual accents upon large and complex patterns of behavior give his poetry a sense of greater depth. Primitive myth and symbol are integral elements of his poetry, as seen in the titles of two of his volumes: *Lupercal* and *Wodwo.* His later volume, *Crow,* shows Hughes moving more consciously in this direction. The crow is a frequent figure representing discord and strife in folk iconography. He is called the Great Crow or Crow Father in both Eskimo legends and in American Indian myths. While the effect is closer to the mythmaking of Yeats or the restructuring of myths by Lawrence, the technique is nearer to Hardy's in *The Dynasts,* where the reader is shown the forces of the world at work, moving both through and beyond the limitations of man.

By his own admission, Gunn's experiments with violence were an existential probing for a fuller commitment to life. When life grinds to a halt, as many felt it had in the 1950s, action itself becomes a symbolic form of commitment; and violent action, an act of intense commitment. As the tempo of life in England and America increased towards the end of the fifties and into the early sixties, Gunn no longer found force and assertion necessary. In his abandonment of this theme we can see the essential difference in the violence explored by the two poets. Gunn, the empiricist, sees violence as an individual act that corresponds to a particular historical and social need; Hughes, the metaphysicist, sees violence as the universal condition of nature in which man partakes along with the rest of animate and inanimate creation. The poetry of Hughes, like that of Yeats and Eliot, is built upon a substructure that is substituted for those universal values that have been displaced from the modern world. It is difficult to say whether such systems will be judged valid or valuable by future generations; however, their worth to poetic expression, in terms of scope and complexity, is very great in the present century.

The confusion that surrounds much of Hughes's poetry derives from what many consider his ambiguous attitude towards violence. Some accuse the poet of advocating some kind of vague indulgence in violence, while others suggest that in his presentation of violence lies an implicit rejection. Hughes himself complicates the matter by his use of an objectifying technique, derived in part from Gerard Manley Hopkins, the Symbolists, and the metaphysical poets, a technique that effectively, to employ Eliot's phrase, lets him escape from emotion and personality.[7] The poet who exposes himself in his poetry opens the possibility of the ultimate destruction of the self (and Hughes could only be too conscious of this from the experience of Sylvia Plath). In addition to the protection against charges of right-wing sympathy to which he might become vulnerable, Hughes sees the artistic technique, again like Eliot and Yeats, as a real and viable refuge for the poetic sensibility. His language, as John Press has observed,[8] attacks the reader with its strength, hardness, and intensity instead of encouraging the reader to enter through the poem into the mind of the poet. As a result of this purposeful seclusion of the personality, critics are only certain of the subject matter (violence) with which Hughes is preoccupied, but encounter greater difficulty when they discuss the poet's attitude towards his material.

We must attempt to understand Hughes by reading many of his poems, for he has a consistent and developing point of view towards violence that emerges through his first four volumes of poetry: *The Hawk in the Rain* (1957), *Lupercal* (1960), *Wodwo* (1967), *Crow* (1971). His primary concern is with violence as a primitive force that is invested in every form of life. It is here that his tone of assertion is present, for the one dominant theme that emerges throughout his poetry is that this mythic violent force is inherent in the very essence of being, from the wind and rocks to humankind. The basic conflict in life revolves on man's attempt to deal with these forces, which on the one hand are subhuman but by that very token are beyond man's capability to subdue. Man must come to terms with this element in his nature, not through suppression or escape (both of which are impossible), but through accommodation. In a sense this demands a Lawrentian "lapsing-out," for man's consciousness and intellect are the basic obstacles to a successful accommodation. Hughes sees the intellect's indulgence in the life of violence as a perversion of the primitive instinct for violence that still persists in the animal world. It is at this point that the poet shows regret for what he sees to be lacking in the modern expression of violence. Violence in nature is actually a positive force, but when man imposes the intellect upon it, he makes it into something destructive. Under these conditions Hughes becomes an apostle against violence. But he emphasizes the distinction and points to the source of the pollution. His emphasis is finally positive with the assertion that man must commit himself to life in spite of what he might consider the destructive consequences of violence upon life.

When Ted Hughes made an adaptation of the Oedipus drama, he chose Seneca's version rather than that of Sophocles because, as he says:

The Greek world saturates Sophocles too thoroughly: the evolution of his play seems complete, fully explored and in spite of its blood-roots, fully civilized. The figures in Seneca's *Oedipus* are Greek only by convention: by nature they are more primitive than aboriginals. They are a spider people, scuttling among hot stones.[9]

In choosing the version that grounded the violence in nature rather than in a particular civilization, Hughes reemphasized the one basic theme that is sounded consistently in his poetry, that violence is an element common to all nature. This is essentially similar to Sylvia Plath's vision as she expressed it in "All the Dead Dears" except that Hughes does not cry out in Kurtz's voice as Plath does: "The horror! The horror!"

"Relic" in fact bears a striking resemblance to "All the Dead Dears," for it too is a poem set in motion through the contemplation of the remains of the dead: "I found this jawbone at the sea's edge." The sea, as is frequently the case in Hughes's poetry, is a Lawrentian blackness in which the primitive forces of instinct and power operate to the exclusion of intelligence and consciousness. In the sea, survival is determined by strength:

> The deeps are cold:
> In that darkness camaraderie does not hold:
> Nothing touches but, clutching, devours.

But this "gross eating game" creates no horror for the poet; rather he accepts it as part of the natural process by which the world renews itself:

> There, crabs, dogfish, broken by the breakers or tossed
> To flap for half an hour and turn to a crust
> Continue the beginning.

"Pike" also displays representatives of this natural world: "Killers from the egg: the malevolent aged grin." The poet is careful to point out the historical associations of the fish, similar to those connected with the bottom of the pond in "To Paint a Water Lily," which from "Prehistoric bedragonned times / Crawl that darkness. . . ." The pike, like the animals of another era, are "a hundred feet long in their world." They also feed upon one another—their lesson is that only the strong and uncompassionate survive: "And indeed they spare nobody." This natural life of violence and cruelty outlasts the highest and noblest achievements of man:

> A pond I fished, fifty yards across,
> Whose lilies and muscular tench
> Had outlasted every visible stone
> Of the monastery that planted them—

What we notice in these earlier poems that tell of violence in the natural world is a direct, sincere voice, the voice of an observer who knows that his detached descriptions are sufficiently effective for his purpose. But the poems in *Crow*, having as their subject a mythical force rather than an actual animal, take on a cynical tone that is echoed in the bitter laughter heard in many of the poems. The poet's vision has crystallized and unified, and the certainty with which he now approaches his theme demands a unique strength.

"Reveille" attempts to explain in a mythical way how man awoke to this violent world, when the serpent, as the source of pain and cruelty, shattered the idealistic dream of Adam and Eve:

> Adam and lovely Eve
> Deep in the first dream
> Each the everlasting
> Holy One of the other
>
> Woke with cries of pain.

Violence, therefore, was part of man's earliest inheritance, and his future was determined by the serpent's curse. His tightening coils crush any hope of a world of innocence, of a world from which violence is absent:

> Behind him, his coils
> Had crushed all Eden's orchards.
> And out beyond Eden
>
> The black, thickening river of his body
> Glittered in giant loops
> Around desert mountains and away
> Over the ashes of the future.

In "Theology," a poem that employs the same biblical myth, the interdestructive forces that were set in motion are more simply and directly outlined:

> Adam ate the apple.
> Eve ate Adam.
> The serpent ate Eve.
> This is the dark intestine.

Alluded to in the title of the earlier poem, "Reveille," is man's summoning or awakening to the same violent life that is common to the rest of nature.

The theme is apparently very important for Hughes, because he returns to it again in *Crow* where he details the horrors of the creation of man rather than recites the narrative in a detached biblical manner. Also the sexual aspects of the story come to the fore in the later account:

> Crow laughed.
> He bit the Worm, God's only son,
> Into two writhing halves.
> He stuffed into man the tail half
> With the wounded end hanging out.

> He stuffed the head half headfirst into woman
> And it crept in deeper and up
> To peer out through her eyes
> Calling its tail-half to join up quickly, quickly
> Because O it was painful.

The violence of love is seen elsewhere as the disfigured offspring of Crow's aborted attempt at love:

> "A final try," said God, "NOW, LOVE."
> . . . .
> And Crow retched again, before God could stop him.
> And woman's vulva dropped over man's neck and tightened.
> The two struggled together on the grass.
> God struggled to part them, cursed, wept—
>
> Crow flew guiltily off.

Similar reverberations of violence are illustrated in the short story "Harvesting" from the volume *Wodwo*. All of nature is locked into an existence by violence; in harvesting, one destroys in order to live. There are various kinds of harvesting that occur in the story: the peasants are cutting the grain in the fields; Grooby, the central character, is hunting rabbits with dogs; the colliers are digging out the hills. When the dogs finally turn upon Grooby and kill him, this is understood as simply another kind of harvesting and the cycle has completed itself.

Hughes's acceptance of life as it is presented in the poems and story described above has brought John Press to describe him aptly as a stoic,[10] for the stoic accepts violence in life and refuses to react to it with horror, contempt, or despair. His response tends to be analytical rather than emotional, and he is more interested in the nature of the violence than in man's reaction to it. The poetry of Hughes is not of the immediate historical moment and as a result is not in as great a danger as that of Gunn and Plath of becoming dated. Even within Gunn's own lifetime readers may forget the connotations of the motorcyclists in the 1950s. But Hughes implants his theme of violence in myth ("Lupercalia," "Wodwo," "Theology") and in animal nature ("Pike," "Thrushes," "Hawk Roosting"). The use of such metaphors in the exploration of his subjects offers an escape from emotional involvement.

Hughes may have learned the need for detachment in reaction to the American poets of the fifties. The limits of their themes and style resulted from their engagement with the immediate social situation. Hughes's response is closer to that of another American poet, Robinson Jeffers, who made a strong plea for emotional withdrawal in the late 1930s:

> I wish you could find the secure value,
> The all-heal I found when a former time hurt me to
> the heart,
> The splendor of inhuman things: you would not be
> looking at each other's throats with your knives.
> ["Air-Raid Rehearsals"]

It is this quality of objective and universal observation that makes one think that Hughes will be the most enduring of these postwar poets. While fully informed by the consciousness of his time and environment, he writes with implications that reach out to all times and all being.

In seeing violence as an historical underpinning of all life, Hughes quickly dismisses the idea of a benevolent nature in favor of images of destructive force. He captures the dissonance of these disparate views in "To Paint a Water Lily." The immediate object of the painter is a traditional romantic scene:

> A green level of lily leaves
> Roofs the pond's chamber.

But the languid description of this almost civilized "chamber" quickly gives way to "the flies' furious arena" in which the dragonfly

> . . . eats meat, . . . bullets by
> Or stands in space to take aim.

While man praises "To see the colours of these flies / Rainbow their arcs,"

> There are battle-shouts
> And death-cries everywhere hereabouts.

These are essentially the same forces at work as in the hawk, the jaguar, the pike, and the thrushes. But the poet does not stop with these immediate elements of the natural world:

> Think what worse
> Is the pond-bed's matter of course.

It is the pond bed from which all living things (including man) have issued, and there "have evolved no improvements there." At the end of "Pike" consciousness of these primitive forces at work in the "stilled legendary depth" of his own being causes fear in the fisherman:

The still splashes on the dark pond,

Owls hushing the floating woods
Frail on my ear against the dream
Darkness beneath night's darkness had freed,
That rose slowly towards me, watching.

The ambiguity of the last participle (does it modify "me" or "darkness"?)
emphasizes the mutuality of the association. The snowdrop, the most fragile,
delicate, and temporary element of nature is a co-sharer of this mindless
cruelty in destroying the mouse, the weasel and the crow:

She, too, pursues her ends,
Brutal as the stars of this month,
Her pale head heavy as metal.
["Snowdrop"]

Man is the creature who has been excluded from the violence of nature,
for his violence is no longer instinctual but planned and intellectualized.
Recognizing this rift between the two worlds of violence, Hughes in poem
after poem sets out mental scouting parties that explore the forms of violence that still link man to the other world: birth, sex, war, and death. He
sees these experiences as means for man to reestablish his connections with
his primitive origins. In "Childbirth" the violence of labor is a link with
the natural world and restores the woman to an almost glorious disorder:

Miracle struck out the brain
Of order and ordinary.

Crag Jack is a representative of the dark world, whose birth and maturation,
in a way analogous to the child in Wordsworth's Immortality Ode, delivered
him from "all the dark churches" that "stooped over my cradle once." The
metaphor of the dark churches is relevant to the larger body of Hughes's
work, since violence is frequently presented in ritualistic terms that subtly
join the violence to man's primitive religious sense. Crag Jack "came clear"
but with the knowledge that

. . . my god's down
Under the weight of all that stone.

It is in the darkness of sleep, the animal world, the earth and sea
his god resides and revelation comes to him through dreams of
His apostasy involves his commitment to the civilized world.

day as opposed to that of night. But he desires to retain his connection
with the dark church, that he might

> Keep more than the memory
> Of a wolf's head, of eagles' feet.

Crag Jack is a symbol of all men who have lost identity with their violent
origins and who have partial insights into their unconscious instincts. Hughes
is frequently preoccupied with examining these insights, always asking if
it is possible, after birth and childhood, to make some kind of accommodation with the violence in his nature. This search provides much of the tension
in his poetry, for the release that he expects to come from indulging the
instincts (in sex, in war) is usually frustrated by the very fact that his
characters are human. He never advocates the abandonment of humanity in
pursuit of one's instincts, and his characters often find it impossible to
straddle the civilized and the instinctual worlds.

One of the connectors that he examines is the sexual union, and the
poet's response is typical of the philosophical dilemma in which he frequently
finds himself. The sexual act, we might expect, should be represented in
his poetry as a viable connection with the instinctual world. But Hughes is
above all honest, and love and sex are seldom positive forces in his work.
Rather it is man's inability to be both man and animal at the same time
that dooms the sexual response. For in accommodating oneself to his
sexual instincts, he submits to a primitive and thoroughly selfish impulse,
or, by avoiding them, he is drawn into ugly repressions.

Hughes's descriptions of male-female relationships are akin to Gunn's,
whose basic metaphor is expressed in the title of *Fighting Terms*. There is
no less violence in Hughes's conception of love, which he expresses in a
two-line image in "The Dove Breeder":

> Love struck into his life
> Like a hawk into a dovecote.

The accommodation with desire is hardly satisfying, for

> Desire's a vicious separator in spite
> Of its twisting women around men. . . .
> ["Incompatibilities"]

The submission to instinct is neither regenerative nor fulfilling. The further
one pursues his passion, the closer he comes to his origins of separateness,
introversion and selfishness:

> Each body still straining to follow down
> The maelstrom dark of the other, their limbs flail
> Flesh and beat upon
> The inane everywhere of its obstacle,
>
> Each, each second, lonelier and further
> Falling alone through the endless
> Without–world of the other, though both here
> Twist so close they choke their cries.

This cynical attitude is further extended in Crow's "Lovesong," which might have been written by D. H. Lawrence or Thom Gunn, for this love song expresses horror at the love which leads to the loss of identity, the possession of one person by another. We might notice the increasing irony of Hughes, as this poem is much later than the former:

> He loved her and she loved him
> His kisses sucked out her whole past or future or tried to
> He had no other appetite
> She bit him she gnawed him she sucked
> She wanted him complete inside her
> Safe and sure forever and ever. . . .

The "Secretary" on the other hand is even more unfulfilled in her refusal to accept any passion into her life. Night and darkness for her are the most terrible times; the instinctual and the unconscious are her greatest enemies. Therefore she

> Goes to bed early, shuts out with the light
> Her thirty years, and lies with buttocks tight,
> Hiding her lovely eyes until day break.

"Macaw and Little Miss" more thoroughly examines man's separation from his primitive origins and his overwhelming desire to reconstruct the connection through the ritual of sex. The macaw symbolizes that primitive element in man that has been trapped "in a cage of wire-ribs / The size of a man's head." The bird, even in its imprisonment, retains its instinctive characteristics, and under such repression he "bristles in a staring / Combustion." In constrast, the aspidistra, a plant that represents all that is genteel and civilized,[11] has been subdued:

> In the old lady's parlour, where an aspidistra succumbs
> To the musk of faded velvet . . .

The poet suggests that the bird has issued from the dark pond of ancient mythology, "a fugitive aristocrat / From some thunderous mythological hierarchy." The old lady's granddaughter, in constant contact with the macaw, feels the strange dark forces at work upon her, awakening her body to instinctual desires and causing her to plead with the moon for fulfillment. She

> lies under every full moon,
> The spun glass of her body bared and so gleam-still
> Her brimming eyes do not tremble or spill
> The dream where the warrior comes, lightning and iron,
> Smashing and burning and rending towards her loin:
> Deep into her pillow her silence pleads.

She feels a strange attraction for the bird, recognizing in him a lost power that she must somehow protect and cherish:

> "Polly. Pretty Poll," she cajoles, and rocks him gently.
> She caresses, whispers kisses. . . .

He, however, closes his eyes to her; he is caged, after all, and tender affection is no means of release for him. It is only when in her total frustration "she strikes the cage in a tantrum and swirls out" that he is aroused; her violence releases his inner forces in a way that her tenderness could not:

> Instantly beak, wings, talons crash
> The bars in conflagration and frenzy,
> And his shriek shakes the house.

War and death are other channels that release the violence of man's animal nature. In "Bayonet Charge" the soldier, under the pressure of battle, abandons the accouterments of culture and civilization, patriotism, heroism, dignity, for the instinctive act of directionless running:

> The patriotic tear that had brimmed in his eye
> Sweating like molten iron from the center of his chest . . .

The distinction between man and animal is man's awareness of his actions, but as he attempts a logical answer to his absurd condition, he receives a sudden vision:

> Then the shot-slashed furrows
> Threw up a yellow hare that rolled like a flame

> And crawled in a threshing circle, its mouth wide
> Open silent, its eyes standing out.

In recognizing his kinship with the wounded rabbit, the soldier abandons even logical thought and gives himself up to instinctive struggle for self-preservation:

> He plunged past with his bayonet toward the green hedge.
> King, honour, human dignity, etcetera
> Dropped like luxuries in a yelling alarm
> To get out of that blue crackling air
> His terror's touchy dynamite.

The violence present in warfare is approached somewhat differently in "Six Young Men," a meditation over a photograph of young smiling soldiers who have since been killed in battle. The poem begins as a traditional war poem, with the ironic contrast between the natural background in the picture that still persists and the human beings that have been destroyed:

> I know
> That bilberried bank, that thick tree, that black wall,
> Which are there yet and not changed.

But then the theme changes; the poet is not so much concerned with how or why men die, but how the violence through which they have died persists in the world. Violence, like the photograph, remains long after the individuals have ceased to exist:

> That man's not more alive whom you confront
> And shake by the hand, see hale, hear speak loud,
> Than any of these six celluloid smiles are,
> Nor prehistoric or fabulous beast more dead;
> No thought so vivid as their smoking blood.
>
> To regard this photograph might well dement,
> Such contradictory permanent horrors here
> Smile from the single exposure and shoulder out
> One's own body from its instant and heat.

The reference to prehistoric and mythical creatures is significant, for it is a common means that Hughes employs to connect all violence. The violence of such creatures (as the violent deaths of the soldiers) in a sense keeps them alive because this inheritance has been passed on through the bonds of violence in all nature. Although prehistoric animals become extinct and dead men rot, the violence remains.

Civilized man is both horrified and afraid of the presence of violence in his world. His means of coping with this violence is to impose more positive values upon it, to classify war as peacekeeping, to describe capital punishment as a crime-deterrent. Whatever might be the method, he forces himself into some kind of retreat in order that he might not see himself as one who employs violence. In "Nicholas Ferrer" this retreat takes the form of traditional religion. The opening image is of the birds who delude themselves by flying away from the darkness "toward an estranged sun." The attempt by Nicholas Ferrer to stop the "weather and dissolution" on the manor farm is analogous to the flight of the birds; both "are more / Ignorant than their charted bones." Family, religion, and intellect are stopgap means to prevent the human from becoming subservient to the nonhuman:

> The farm, the church and Nicholas' frontal bone
> Walled out a clouded world. . . .

But as the birds could not hold off the darkness, Nicholas is unable to prevent the decay of human and divine values; with his death these values once again disappear:

> And again the fire of God
> Is under the shut heart, under the grave sod.

In similar fashion the nonhuman overcomes man's endeavors in "October Dawn." The onset of winter, calling to mind the world's earlier periods, erases the traces left by a party on the previous evening:

> The lawn overtrodden and strewn
> From the night before, and the whistling green
> Shrubbery are doomed. Ice
> Has got its spearhead into place.

The struggle between the human and inhuman is more fully examined in "Thistles." Man's progress (hoeing) and nature's tranquillity (cows) are thwarted by nature's stronger primitive powers:

> Against the rubber tongues of cows and the hoeing hands of men
> Thistles spike the summer air.

The thistles, representatives of an earlier age when man lived more by his instincts, have survived like "pale hair and the gutturals of dialects":

Every one a revengeful burst
Of resurrection, a grasped fistful
Of splintered weapons and Icelandic frost thrust up

From the underground stain of a decayed Viking.

Though the thistles themselves, like man, are limited by their impermanence
—"Then they grow grey, like men"—man is hostile towards them because
they recall to him elements of his nature that he would rather forget; therefore he tries to destroy them: "Mown down, it is a feud." But the two
elements, the civilized and the primitive, continue in their offspring, and
the battle is waged anew:

> Their sons appear,
> Stiff with weapons, fighting back over the same ground.

Hughes seldom draws sketches of those who successfully join battle
against the powers represented by the thistles, although Nicholas Ferrer
and the secretary fight to a standstill. More often he shows the human
element being bested by the nonhuman in some violent confrontation, as
in "Bayonet Charge" or "The Green Wolf." The latter poem centers on
the approaching death of a man paralyzed on one side. It is out of a "dark
heaven" that the murderous bloodclot approaches. But death here is not a
negation, for it is the flowering of natural forces that brings on this death;
for this reason, "You watch it approaching but you cannot fear it." The
last stanza recalls the linguistic impact and metaphysical message of Dylan
Thomas's "The Force That through the Green Fuse Drives the Flower":

> That star
> And that flower and that flower
> And living mouth and living mouth all
>
> One smouldering annihilation
> Of old brains, old bowels, old bodies.
> In the scarves of dew, the wet hair of nightfall.

Hughes's most successful exposition of this struggle between the human
and nonhuman, or the instinctive and civilized, is in "Ghost Crabs."[12] The
crabs emerge at night from the dark world of the sea, true representatives
of Lawrentian darkness:

> At nightfall, as the sea darkens,
> A depth darkness thickens, mustering from the gulfs
>   and submarine badlands,
> To the sea's edge.

A close familiarity with Hughes's poetry will reveal the wide extent to which he employs images of the night, darkness, and sea to represent the irrational and instinctive element of nature. For instance, the crabs, coming to the land at night, recall the impersonal force of warfare:

> Giant crabs, under flat skulls, staring inland
> Like a packed trench of helmets.

Man considers himself secure against the ugly realities that the crabs represent, and he is taken unaware as the crabs invade his sanctuaries:

> Our walls, our bodies, are no problem to them.
> ....
> [they] Press through our nothingness where we sprawl on our beds,
> Or sit in our rooms.

The immediate reaction is to clear the houses of these creatures, denying all association between our world and theirs. But our nightmare, which is not a dream but reality, tells us that the two worlds are one:

> Or we jerk awake to the world of our possessions
> With a gasp, in a sweat burst, brains jamming blind
> Into the bulb-light. Sometimes, for minutes, a sliding
> Staring
> Thickness of silence
> Presses between us. These crabs own this world.

Their actions are the ordinary human actions of using, attacking, abusing, and destroying others, an order that once again recalls Plath's "gross eating game." In fact, what drives the crabs is what inspires the great and powerful men of this world:

> All night, around us or through us,
> They stalk each other, they fasten on to each other,
> They mount each other, they tear each other to pieces,
> They utterly exhaust each other.
> They are the powers of this world.

At dawn the crabs return to the sea, and man is free to pursue his idealistic course once more. Although they remain invisible, they determine the violence and horror of man's history:

> They are the turmoil of history, the convulsion
> In the roots of blood, in the cycles of concurrence.

They are, finally, "God's only toys." For his amusement God allows the crabs (man's instincts) to run wild, and the world is thrown into turmoil. The crabs lead to war, hatred, power and corruption, and violence.

Again we must turn to the poems in *Crow* to see these ideas more fully developed. There is constant tension and confrontation between man's intelligence and the powers represented by Crow. Hughes sees one of man's basic failings to be his continuous effort to objectify "evil," or in Crow's amoral world, the black forces. "Crow's Account of St. George" is one of the most horrifying poems about human relationships in our language. It begins with the premise that man is misdirected in attempting to see a logical order in the universe:

> He sees everything in the Universe
> Is a track of numbers racing towards an answer.

Because of this orderly universe, he is led to believe he can control and master those elements that he finds hostile, as the early Christians in England invented a Saint George to do battle with the projected evil, the dragon. The mistake soon becomes evident; by projecting the evil outside man, it remains undetected as it grows within and around him. Once he begins to search out evil, he encounters it everywhere–the blackness is omnipresent. His struggle to destroy the evil should only be told in the language of the poem:

> Now with a shriek
> An object four times bigger than the others–
> A belly-ball of hair, with crab-legs, eyeless,
> Jabs its pincers into his face,
> Its belly opens–a horrible oven of fangs,
> The claws are clawing to drag him towards it–
> He snatches from its mount on the wall a sword,
> A ceremonial Japanese decapitator,
> And as hacking a path through thicket he scatters
> The lopped segments, the opposition collapses.
> He stands trousered in blood and log-splits
> The lolling body, bifurcates it
> Top to bottom, kicks away the entrails–
> Steps out of the blood-wallow.

The primal battle must be seen in part as sexual if we read these lines closely. But more than that, the point is that once we seek the abodes of evil, it will force us to destroy those to whom we are closest:

> Recovers–
> Drops the sword and runs dumb-faced from the house
> Where his wife and children lie in their blood.

Man does not live in a controlled and controllable world, and his intelligence is not adequate to bring him through whole: "Humankind cannot bear too much reality."

Because man has become isolated from what Hughes sees as his true nature, the poet offers for a solution an accommodation with his violent nature that depends upon his ability to fuse the intellectual and instinctual. All attempts to overcome the outbreaks of violence from below result either in defeat for the human element ("Two Wise Generals") or at best in a stand-still that promises continuing struggle in the future ("Thistles"). Since there seems to be no danger of man's abandoning intellect and consciousness, Hughes directs his attention to an accommodation that man must make with the instinctual part of his nature. In the effort to achieve this balance, he must abandon himself to or at least consent to the violent forces within him and accept his consciousness not as a help in this matter but as a burden. He seeks a way to relieve the tensions of poems like "Secretary" and "Incompatibilities," tensions that frequently result in unresolved frustrations. He recognizes the validity of submitting to the destructive element, while at the same time realizing the necessity of emerging as a whole human being. Two sides of this essential problem are explored in the title poems of *The Hawk in the Rain* and *Wodwo*. The former shows the man caught between the two forces and unable to resolve the tension; the latter depicts a symbolic accommodation that releases this tension.

"The Hawk in the Rain" is a good example of an animal poem whose real focus is upon man. The speaker of the poem opens with the narrative "I," emphasizing both the point of view in the poem and the focus of attention. For it is this man's consciousness that is his burden—caught between the muddy earth that drags him down and his human consciousness that urges him onward and upward, this hybrid creature is in the process of being destroyed by the demands of these two forces:

> I drown in the drumming ploughland, I drag up
> Heel after heel from the swallowing of the earth's mouth,
> From clay that clutches my each step to the ankle
> With the habit of the dogged grave. . . .

His examination of the situation is to a great extent what makes it unbearable for the human, for it forces him to continue his frenetic motions of escape. Contrasted to this panicky creature is the hawk, whose stillness and lack of consciousness signal his triumph over the world:

> . . . but the hawk
> Effortlessly at height hangs his still eye.

His "still eye" finds other equivalents in the poem: "the diamond point of will" and "the master fulcrum of violence." The hawk encompasses all three qualities; man is seldom capable of this, but at times achieves one of these qualities in his abandonment of consciousness in a purely instinctive attempt to hold on to life:

> ... the hawk hangs
> The diamond point of will that polestars
> The sea drowner's endurance.

This strikingly recalls the poem "Lerici" by Thom Gunn, in which he praises unconscious and fruitless violence:

> Strong swimmers, fishermen, explorers: such
> Dignify death by thriftless violence–
> Squandering all their little left to spend.

The hawk, riding effortlessly on the winds of the storm, symbolizes the accommodation and commitment to violence that one must make in order to survive. Such commitment places one at the fulcrum of violence which is a still point, a moment that frees one from consciousness to look upon a situation objectively without being caught up in it, "the resolution of its partial horror." Man in his conscious resistance to the storm stands away from the center and suffers the more for it:

> ... banging wind kills these stubborn hedges,
>
> Thumbs my eyes, throws my breath, tackles my heart,
> And rain hacks my head to the bone ...

It is only the finality of death that can blot out man's consciousness and thus bring him into harmony with nature, where he can, like the hawk, like a drowning swimmer, struggle valiantly against the rain. His efforts under such conditions balance him on the same still point that the hawk occupies:

> ... and I,
>
> Bloodily grabbed dazed last-moment-counting
> Morsel in the earth's mouth, strain towards the master-
> Fulcrum of violence where the hawk hangs still.

There is, however, no illusion of lasting peace. The hawk too will eventually meet destruction, but it will be with the dignity of one who rides his body furiously to death:

That maybe in his own time meets the weather

Coming the wrong way, suffers the air, hurled upside down,
Fall from his eye, the ponderous shires crash on him,
The horizon trap him; the round angelic eye
Smashed, mix his heart's blood with the mire of the land.

This same idea reappears in the much later poem "Gnat-Psalm," in which
the gnats achieve an almost angelic beauty through their feverish acceptance
of death:

> O little Hasids
> Ridden to death by your own bodies
> Riding your bodies to death
> You are the angels of the only heaven!

In contrast to the fully civilized man whose consciousness is his burden,
"Wodwo" presents a creature who is half-man, half-animal, and who balances his conscious world against his instinctive self. The wodwo is one
who can descend to his primitive roots as well as ascend to intellectual
heights. The quotation from *Sir Gawain and the Green Knight* with which
Hughes prefaces *Wodwo* emphasizes the versatility of man and his connections, not only with the gods but also with prehistoric creatures and half-men:

> Sumwhyle wyth wormez he werrez, and wyth wolves als,
> Sumwhyle wyth wodwos, that woned in the knarrez,
> Bothe wyth bullez and berez, and borez otherquyle,
> And etaynez, that hym anelede of the heze felle.

The wodwo is not a purely instinctive creature, for his prime concern is
philosophical: "What am I?" His answer, however, does not look to the
gods; rather he goes back to the source of life: "I enter water." As he swims
in the water, touching neither the river bottom nor the air above, he feels
the dilemma of one straddling two worlds:

> What am I to split
> The glassy grain of water looking upward I see the bed
> Of the river above me upside down very clear
> What am I doing here in mid-air?

It is not only the world that he finds topsy-turvy but also his place in this
world. His struggle for consciousness and identity is paralleled by his
attempt to formulate his thoughts in adequate phrases. But his fluid primitive language reflects his still fluid position in the world, for his consciousness has not defined him in such a way as to make him static. Like the poet,

the wodwo inspects the animal kingdom hoping to find clues to his own nature:

> Why do I find
> this frog so interesting as I inspect its most secret
> interior and make it my own?

His most vigorous intellectual attempts are directed towards understanding the freedom of his instinctive nature, as again Hughes the poet uses his intelligence to explore the role of man's instinct:

> I seem
> separate from the ground and not rooted but dropped
> out of nothing casually I've no threads
> fastening me to anything I can go anywhere
> I seem to have been given the freedom
> of this place what am I then?

In trying to understand his nature, the wodwo realizes that it has connections with primitive evolutionary forces that are beyond his understanding; yet he resolves to continue his search:

> I suppose I am the exact centre
> but there's all this what is it roots
> roots roots roots and here's the water
> again very queer but I'll go on looking

Hughes would say that, unfortunately, the consciousness of modern man does not lead him back to nature as in "Wodwo," but it knowingly destroys the world from which man has evolved, making the necessary return impossible:

> The hot shallows and seas we bring our blood from
> Slowly dwindled; cooled
> To sewage estuary, to trout-stocked tarn.

Man not only despoils nature in the attempt to cover his traces, but he wages a dual battle upon his own intelligence. The creative element of the mind is destroyed, so that it only reacts in an artificial, controlled manner, what the poet might mockingly consider the height of intellectual sophistication:

> Now the mind's wandering elementals,
> Ousted from their traveller-told

> Unapproachable islands,
> From their heavens and their burning underworld,
> Wait dully at the traffic crossing,
> Or lean over headlines, taking nothing in.

A similar separation from nature is seen in "November." Dark winter is approaching, ushered in by a cold November rain. The speaker cuts himself off from these crude forces both physically, by his boots, and philosophically by his consciousness, which assures him that summer shall return. But the security of his isolation is jarred when he sees a tramp whom he takes for dead sleeping in a ditch:

> But his stillness separated from the death
> Of the rotting grass and the ground.

The stillness that the tramp achieves is cousin to the stillness of the hawk, attained through accommodation with these forces. But the observer, while admiring the tramp's trust, is unable to commit himself to the natural world and runs away. However, he discovers some animals caught in a keeper's gibbet, owls, hawks, weasels, cats, crows. In their exposure to the elements, he sees a parallel to the tramp's sleep:

> Some still had their shape,
> Had their pride with it; hung, chins on chests,
> Patient to outwait these worst days that beat
> Their crowns bare and dripped from their feet.

The theme of man's separation from nature and instinct appears frequently in Hughes's poetry, and although the immediate concern of many of the poems is not violence, he repeatedly emphasizes that violence is one of the natural forces with which man has lost contact, and as a result has suffered some damage to his natural soul. It is a small philosophical step from "Fourth of July," in which Hughes decries man's moving away from his origins, to "Mayday on Holderness," in which he describes man's continuing connections. In this poem the violently selfish nature of being is accentuated through juxtaposition with an apparently sympathetic and friendly world: "This evening, motherly summer moves in the pond." But like the river Humber, which "drains the effort of the inert North," man is also prepared to feed off others:

> Birth-soils,
> The sea-salts, scoured me, cortex and intestine,
> To receive these remains.

Only unconsciousness makes man capable of living in such a world: "Flower-like, I loved nothing." No wonder that "Dead and unborn are in God comfortable," for only they escape this continuing parasitism. Man, who has not escaped, shares his nature with the most vicious and brutal of the animal world:

> What a length of gut is growing and breathing—
> This mute eater, biting through the mind's
> Nursery floor, with eel and hyena and vulture,
> With creepy-crawly and the root,
> With the sea-worm, entering its birthright.

In the darkness of night, the sexuality of man is analogous to the promiscuous destruction of the animal world:

> The crow sleeps glutted and the stoat begins.
> There are eye-guarded eggs in the hedgerows,
> Hot haynests under the roots in burrows.
> Couples at their pursuits are laughing in the lanes.

But Hughes is not always so cynical in his approach to violence. Man is unable to renounce totally his consciousness, and his burden therefore is to employ his intelligence in the service of his violent nature. The thrust of violence can be positive or negative; in "The Martyrdom of Bishop Farrar" the poet's metaphysical concern with violence finds a workable metaphor that stresses the revitalizing powers of violent action, reminiscent of Gunn's "Mirror for Poets" and "Claus von Stauffenberg." Queen Mary and her men are seen as destructive agents of violence:

> Bloody Mary's venomous flames can curl;
> They can shrivel sinew and char bone
> Of foot, ankle, knee, and thigh, and boil
> Bowels, and drop his heart a cinder down;
> And her soldiers can cry, as they hurl
> Logs in the red rush: "This is her sermon."

But Farrar is a man acquainted with violence, one who will not flinch before it. He is not the kind to advise his followers to shy away from Mary because she employs brutal methods; rather they must come to terms with the violence turned upon them. Those who try to escape these forces are destroyed:

> So it might have been: seeing their exemplar
> And teacher burned for his lessons to black bits,

> Their silence might have disowned him to her,
> And hung up what he had taught with their Welsh hats:
> Who sees his blasphemous father struck by fire
> From heaven, might well be heard to speak no oaths.

Farrar, however, embraces the violence and employs it for his own purposes rather than for Mary's. He had said, "If I flinch from the pain of the burning, believe not the doctrine that I have preached." And so "he fed his body to the flame alive." The ambiguity of the last word asserts the revitalizing and fulfilling power of undergoing this torture. It not only assured the bishop dignity and honor in death (cf. "Gnat-Psalm," "The Hawk in the Rain") but also guaranteed the continuance of his teachings among his followers:

> When they saw what annuities of hours
> And comfortable blood he burned to get
> His words a bare honouring in their ears,
> The shrewd townsfolk pocketed them hot:
> Stamp was not current but they rang and shone
> As good gold as any queen's crown.

The position of Bishop Farrar in this poem is not very different from that of Hughes in his role as poet. Preaching a lesson of man's basic brutality and the necessity for accommodation with this part of one's nature, he must necessarily come into conflict with traditional social values. But his success as poet does not rest in his retreat from violence but in exploring this as his theme. The poet finds greater credibility among his readers not in avoiding this issue (like the neohumanists) but in pursuing the study of violence in man's nature. Those who try to frighten people away from violence are guilty of leading people astray: "An ignorant means to establish ownership / Of his flock!"

Those who try to escape the implications of living in a violent world are generally shown to be failures. Man may attempt to substitute wisdom, shrewdness, ideals of brotherhood, for the forces of his violent nature, but his attempts prove futile. In "Two Wise Generals" these old shrewd military leaders meet to settle their differences by discussion and treaty rather than by battle:

> "Not as Black Douglas, bannered, trumpeted,
> Who hacked for the casked heart flung to the enemy,
> Letting the whole air flow breakneck with blood
> Till he fell astride that handful, you and I
>
> Come, two timid and ageing generals
> To parley, and to divide the territory

Upon a map, and get honour, and by
This satisfaction part with regiments whole."

Ironically, these two wise old men think they eliminate man's natural ferocity
by signing a piece of paper. One simple civilized act to wipe out centuries of
animal viciousness. But this very act exposes their own inability to escape
that rapacious nature: "lands allotted (and a good third / Stuffed down
their tunic fronts' private estate)." It should be no surprise to them when
they return home at dawn and

> Both
> Have found their sleeping armies massacred.

What has been illustrated through anecdote in "Two Wise Generals" is
explained further through paradigm in "Law in the Country of the Cats."
Man would like to think he is governed by rational, civilized law which supports ideals of brotherhood and love of neighbor. For when hatred then
enters into his relationships, he can explain it rationally from a social or
cultural point of view: the natural animosity between "beggar-man and
rich man," "Cuckold-maker and cuckold," "Bully and delicate boy." But
Hughes explodes the notion of brotherhood, and describes a different kind
of hatred that is not dependent upon one's cultural environment:

> When two men meet for the first time in all
> Eternity and outright hate each other,
> . . . .
> As dog and wolf because their blood before
> They are aware has bristled into their hackles. . . .

These men are not responsive to human law but to more primitive urgings
to violence that deny humanistic ideals:

> . . . facts have sacked
> The oath of the pious witness who judged all men
> As a one humble brotherhood of man.

Although upon meeting, their first civilized reaction might be to discuss

> "universal brotherhood,"
> "Love of humanity and each fellow-man,"
> Or "the growing likelihood of perpetual peace,"

consciousness will soon give way before catlike instinct and "then a flash
of violent incredible action. . . ."

The cat image returns and is enlarged in "Of Cats," where the poet describes man's basic emotions in these terms:

> A heart constituted wholly of cats
> . . . .
> From father and mother a child inherits.

Man tries to repress or destroy this part of his nature (through humanistic directives?), but it is a hopeless task. A man who tried to drown a cat one night "Found that cat on the doorstep waiting for him." Escape and repression, although frequently attempted, are futile means of dealing with one's catlike nature: "So are we all held in utter mock by the cats."

Neohumanistic philosophy fails in refusing to acknowledge the "dark intestine" that is man's destiny. Frustration seems to be the tone of a number of poems illustrating the theme of man's destructive nature, the frustration being barely controlled by a poet who feels his audience does not dare to listen to him. "Criminal Ballad" presents the education of what Hughes would consider the romantic humanist, the man who insists on defending his vision of a happy world. But as he vigorously protests the beauty of the world, this very act bloodies his hands, marks his participation in the destructive acts he struggled against. His initial response is to weep for the loss of his imagined world, until he realizes that the real world is absurd and cruel, and nothing he will do can change it; so "he began to laugh." This is a difficult lesson to have set before us, but Hughes insists that we face the situation nakedly. In this sense, his poetry becomes a rending of the veil, the veil of illusion that allows us to remain in happy contact with nature, with our fellow men, with ourselves. Any attempt to alter this reality, or any effort to contend with the dark forces is futile and ridiculous—the traditional concept of the mythic hero who might come to destroy the black force and make the world safe for mankind is absurd. "The Contender" who devotes his life to this crusade has in the end only "his senseless trial of strength" as his reward.

It is also obvious from the tone of many of these poems that Hughes is keenly aware of the polarity of his own vision with that of traditional humanists. At times, indeed, such humanistic impulses become his antagonist as he is tempted to avoid all contact with the dark and to abandon his more instinctive urgings to submit to his destiny. This tension and opposition is metaphorically examined in a very Lawrentian poem, "A Dream of Horses." Our conscious educated psyches are the stabled horses that consume all our time:

> All our wealth horse-dung and the combings of horses,
> And all we can talk about is what horses ail.

But while we are imprisoned by the concerns of the conscious world, the wild horses outside the stable tempt us to come forth and submit to them:

> We crouched at our lantern, our bodies drank the din,
> And we longed for a death trampled by such horses
> As every grain of the earth had hooves and mane.

These horses not only recall the violent, sexual powers of Robinson Jeffers's "Roan Stallion"[13] but also D. H. Lawrence, who in *Fantasia of the Unconscious* says that a dream of horses surging about an individual indicates that "the spontaneous self is secretly yearning for the liberation and fulfillment of the deepest and most powerful sensuous nature."[14] In addition, the scene in *The Rainbow* in which Ursula is almost trampled by the horses finds its parallel in "The Rain Horse," a short story in *Wodwo*. Both Ursula Brangwen and "the young man" in Hughes's story experience the purgation of their consciousness. After her experience with the horses, Ursula

sat there, spent, time and the flux of change passed away from her, she lay as if unconscious upon the bed of the stream, like a stone, unconscious, unchanging, unchangeable, whilst everything rolled by in transience, leaving her there, a stone at rest on the bed of the stream, inalterable and passive, sunk to the bottom of all change.[15]

The young man in "The Rain Horse," having been disillusioned with his earlier romantic view of nature, "just sat staring at the ground, as if some important part had been cut out of his brain." It is the exact position of Crow, whose countless efforts to change natural objects into positive force result only in destruction. Knowledge of truth brings Crow's actions into harmony with the world: "Crow / Never again moved." In "A Dream of Horses" also, the dream is not strong enough to seduce the men out of themselves, and they wake to the realities of the modern world and their still-imprisoned selves: ". . . our stable-horses / Lay in their straw, in a hag-sweat, listless and wretched."

The woman in "Lupercalia" similarly seeks release from the sterility of the world through subjection to the forces represented by the goats and dog. Violent purification brings her into the circle of the quick:

> . . . the dog has blessed
> Their fury. Fresh thongs of goat-skin
> In their hands they go bounding past,
> And deliberate welts have snatched her in
>
> To the figure of racers.

Those who are able to accommodate themselves to the violence in nature begin with a certain crudeness in their souls (e.g., the tramp in "November," "Wodwo") or live in a more primitive age (the woman in "Lupercalia"). The greatest difficulty is encountered by the man most conscious of his human role, the intellectual. Hughes explores this man's attempt to reconcile his torn consciousness, and he is found unable to cope with the violent side of his nature. The two aspects of man are seen in "November," in which the intellectual element stares with horror at that part of humanity, the tramp, who is able to sleep unconsciously in the wet ditch. His rubber boots effectively protect him from the rain, but he is more frightened in his awareness than the sleeping trustful tramp, and runs away. The intellectual is even more incapable of success when he encounters these forces directly, as in "Strawberry Hill." The stoat, a predatory animal, dances before men, "the maskers," who are trying to disguise the fact that they are partaking in the same dance. The stoat is greater than both their intellectual and physical guards; he "bit / Through grammar and corset." They can kill the animal— "they nailed to a door / The stoat with the sun in its belly"—but they are unable to escape his lesson:

> But its red unmanageable life
> Has licked the stylist out of their skulls. . . .

Man thinks that his intellect controls his world, but his predatory nature devours an age, "has sucked that age like an egg and gone off," only to emerge again in some faraway place or even somewhere very near: "Emerges thirsting, in far Asia, in Brixton." The cats, Hughes tells us elsewhere, possess the night, and our educated sensibilities are unable to cope with them: "They have outwitted our nimblest wits" ("Of Cats").

Intellect, of course, is equated with progress. But ironically that very progress has stunted its own origins. In "Fourth of July," with its obvious reference to American culture, progress is the cause of destruction:

> Columbus' huckstering breath
> Blew inland through North America
>
> Killing the last of the mammoths.

But Columbus, the symbol of commercial man here, has destroyed the world of natural power and has cut himself off from instinct and initiative:

> Now the mind's wandering elementals,
> . . . .
> Wait dully at the traffic crossing,
> Or lean over headlines, taking nothing in.

Man should surrender his mental faculties to more primitive urgings, like
the gnats:

> Not writing and not fighting but singing
> That the cycles of this Universe are no matter
> That they are not afraid of the sun
> That the one sun is too near
> It blasts their song, which is of all the suns
> That they are their own sun. . . .

And whether the thinking man admits it or not, death will reduce him to
what his intellect fought against in life:

> Whether you say it, think it, know it
> Or not, it happens, it happens, as
> Over rails over
> The neck the wheels leave
> The head with its vocabulary useless,
> Among the flogged plantains.

The most incriminatory description of the intellectual's attempt to deal
with raw nature appears in "Egg-Head." The egghead is an observer who
reacts intellectually to life, without ever soiling his soul with experience.
He shields himself in a "militant pride" rather than indulge in a nature
against which is needed

> the freebooting crass
> Veterans of survival and those champions
> Forgetfulness, madness.

Prudence, not passion, inspires the egghead to "shut out the world's knock-
ing / With a welcome." He is shut off both actively and passively from the
powers of the world:

> Long the eggshell head's
> Fragility rounds and resists receiving the flash
> Of the sun, the bolt of the earth.

Instead, he overcomes his helplessness to deal with the real world

> By feats of torpor, by circumventing sleights
> Of stupefaction, juggleries of benumbing,
> By lucid sophistries of sight. . . .

His pin- / Point cipher" and "blank-stare courtesy" are means of avoiding

life rather than confronting it; his own insignificant intellectual processes
effectively seal him off from vital contacts:

> . . . opposing his eye's flea-red
> Fly-catching fervency to the whelm of the sun,
> Trumpet his own ear dead.

At the most, primitive forces like the wind that represent violent movement
shove his conscious mental preoccupations to the background and paralyze
his intellect:

> Now deep
> In chairs, in front of the great fire, we grip
> Our hearts and cannot entertain book, thought,
>
> Or each other.

Although Hughes sees the attempted escape from violence as an escape
from life, and the intellectual's circumvention as a sign of weakness and ineffectual temporizing, he never assumes an assertive stance that indiscriminately approves of all violent acts. Hughes seldom creates circumstances
that lend themselves to a strong criticism of violence, but there are several
striking poems in which this occurs. From these poems we understand what
he finds offensive in the modern expression of violence and how he feels
an essentially healthy instinct has been perverted in modern history.

His basic complaint is that modern violence has ceased to be a function
of those instinctive urgings that he writes about in most of his poetry. "The
Ancient Heroes and the Bomber Pilot" contrasts ancient and modern wielder
of violence, stressing that what is lacking in the pilot is the sense of personal
self-expression in his acts so that they become totally destructive both in
reference to himself and to his victims. The ancient heroes on the other
hand found healthy expression in their violent acts:

> They thinned down their fat fulsome blood in war,
> Replenishing both bed and board,
>
> Making their own good news, restuffing their dear
> Fame with fresh sacks-full of heads,
> Roaring, burdened, back over the wet moor.

These men were driven by instinct, not intellect, and

> Got nowhere by sitting still
> To hear some timorous poet enlarge heroisms,
> To suffer their veins stifle and swell—

The bomber pilot, on the other hand, is a highly sophisticated instrument of war, trained to kill by command, not from need or desire. Contrasting his own actions and motives with his ancient counterparts, he is mortified: "The grandeur of their wars humbles my thought." His destruction is vaster and more certain, but he kills unknowingly and impersonally; his violence is of a different kind:

> Even though I can boast
> The enemy capital will jump to a fume
> At a turn of my wrist
>
> And the huge earth be shaken in its frame,–
> I am pale.
> When I imagine one of those warriors in the room
>
> And hear his heart-beat burl
> The centuries are a stopped clock; my heart
> Is cold and small.

"Wilfred Owen's Photographs" expresses a similar theme. Parliament, considering whether to abolish the British navy's cat-o-nine tails, "squared against the motion." This civilized body of contemporary men had no trouble consenting to the use of a primitive instrument of violence as long as the argument was concerned with a removed, impersonal object:

> "To discontinue it were as much
> As ship not powder and cannonballs
> But brandy and women" (Laughter).

But an Irishman brings a "cat" into the chambers and watches "the gentry fingering its stained tails." Those who were able to deal intellectually with the abstract issue of violent punishment are unable to cope emotionally with the immediate bloody instrument:

> Whereupon . . .
>   quietly, unopposed,
> The motion was passed.

Nor is man greatly concerned with individual suffering and violence. In "A Woman Unconscious" man's modern consciousness is preoccupied with universal destruction, which is a substitute for his concern with private tragedy. It is no longer a question of one warrior fighting another ("The Ancient Heroes and the Bomber Pilot") but "Russia and America circle each other." The possibility of total destruction, "the world-cancelling black," accentuates man's growing concern with impersonal forces of violence and his disregard of the immediate. The bomber pilot could make the enemy capital "jump to a fume," but he would be insensible to the suffering of the thousands burned alive. Hughes seriously challenges this loss of values in an atomic age, and cries out with more immediate passion than is usual in his poetry:

> And though bomb be matched against bomb,
> Though all mankind wince out and nothing endure—
> Earth gone in an instant flare—
> Did a lesser death come
>
> Onto the white hospital bed
> Where one, numb beyond her last of sense,
> Closed her eyes on the world's evidence
> And into pillows sunk her head.

A different and stranger lament for these changing values is recorded by Hughes in "The Retired Colonel." This poem has undesirable associations with the poetry of Kipling, the most dangerous element in Thom Gunn (his praise of unthinking activists in "Lines from a Book"), and the somewhat panicky reactions of the Angry Young Men to England's reduced stature after World War II. The poem is a eulogy for the strong military type who

> Barked at his dog knout and whipcrack
> And cowerings of India: five or six wars
> Stiffened in his reddened neck. . . .

He, the last of an old guard, "would not go down / While posterity's trash stood." In a tone that is a mixture of terror and alarm, the poet asks, "And what if his sort should vanish?" In an answer that might well recall the reactionary Pound or Yeats, he asserts that the world will be given over to the rabble; the strong individual will be overcome by the hording masses: "The man-eating British lion / By a pimply age brought down." Through images that recur in other of his poems, Hughes gives a better idea of his intention in the last stanza:

> Here's his head mounted, though only in rhymes,
> Beside the head of the last English
> Wolf . . .
> And the last sturgeon of Thames.

Modern society dismisses the values represented by the colonel, the wolf, the sturgeon, but the poet has taken it upon himself to preserve these, at least in his poetry. One must recall poems like "February," "Lupercalia," and "Pike" in which wolves and fish are symbols of those violent primitive forces that are being lost in the modern world. In "February" it is Hughes himself, the poet of violence, who wears a wolf mask:

> Under severe moons he sits making
> Wolf-masks, mouths clamped well onto the world.

The colonel, in his Victorian assertiveness, is a human representative of power, and Hughes accordingly bemoans his exit from the stage. If this is the mask, "face pulped scarlet with kept rage," behind which the poet thinks the human spirit should involve itself in natural violence, the connotations are sinister indeed. We might only hope that if the ancient heroes were resurrected, they would appear under the guise neither of the bomber pilot nor of the British colonel in India. In contrasting the lion to the rabble, Hughes is forcing a choice upon us that is unnecessary; if his sort should disappear, it does not necessarily follow that "The rabble starlings roar upon / Trafalgar." However, this poem appears to be a momentary swerving to an extreme that is not confirmed by his work at large.

There is something paradoxical in illustrating elements of misguided violence through such disparate portraits as those of the retired colonel and the unconscious woman. But in both cases there is a pessimistic tone with regard to contemporary society that raises both moral and practical questions. If Hughes sees man's nature as essentially violent, but at the same time condemns the expressions of violence in his contemporary historical environment, what alternatives are left open to the poet? They appear to be threefold: 1) abandon the investigation in frustration, as Gunn had done; 2) abandon life in despair, as Plath had done; or 3) crusade against violence, as the neohumanistic poets do. Hughes fortunately does not lock himself into any of these responses, each of which in its own way is an easy solution to the dilemma in which the poet finds himself. While registering the frustration, the despair, and the moral indignation, Hughes never retreats from what the majority of his poems describe as man's commitment to life, his association with primitive nature. His final accents are positive, for Hughes asserts that the human spirit, not only in spite of the violence of its nature, but also because of it, must always turn towards life, never away from life.

Hughes quite clearly expresses this part of his philosophy in a short three-stanza poem that is almost lost in the middle of *The Hawk in the Rain:* "Invitation to the Dance." This is an extremely important poem in a discussion of Hughes's attitude towards violence, for while acknowledging that the essence of life is touched with violence and brutality, it asserts that these elements should not deter us from committing ourselves to a full and active participation in life.

INVITATION TO THE DANCE

The condemned prisoner stirred, but could not stir:
Cold had shackled the blood-prints of the knout.
The light of his death's dawn put the dark out.
He lay, his lips numb to the frozen floor.
He dreamed some other prisoner was dragged out—
Nightmare of command in the dawn, and a shot.
The bestial gaoler's boot was at his ear.

Upon his sinews torturers had grown strong,
The inquisitor old against a tongue that could not,
Being torn out, plead even for death.
All bones were shattered, the whole body unstrung.
Horses, plunging apart towards North and South,
Tore his heart up by the shrieking root.
He was flung to the blow-fly and the dog's fang.

Pitched onto his mouth in a black ditch
All spring he heard the lovers rustle and sigh.
The sun stank. Rats worked at him secretly.
Rot and maggot stripped him stitch by stitch.
Yet still this dream engaged his vanity:
That could he get upright he would dance and cry
Shame on every shy or idle wretch.   [italics mine]

This poem focuses for Hughes a major thematic direction, very much the same way (thematically and morally) that "Ulysses" did for Tennyson. The prisoner here is dying of torture and putrefaction, while Ulysses is growing old, experiencing perhaps the ultimate violence of life. Man is not paralyzed by his disuse, but by his fear of participating in a world scarred by violence. The dreadful cell that the prisoner inhabits is the society of greed and power that Orwell describes in *1984;* the first stanza is parallel to Orwell's picture of the future: "If you want a picture of the future, imagine a boot stamping on a human face—forever." Not only is he being destroyed, but part of his torture is a preclusion of the desire to escape from his violent world:

Upon his sinews torturers had grown strong,
The inquisitor old against a tongue that could not,
Being torn out, plead even for death.

The natural forces of the world join themselves to human malice to hasten his dissolution:

The sun stank. Rats worked at him secretly.
Rot and maggot stripped him stitch by stitch.

What finally is the response of one who has undergone such violence to those who refuse to enter the dance, who fearfully or smugly isolate themselves from life with despairing or humanistic excuses? Ted Hughes, the poet who knowingly inhabits a violent world, might at this point be speaking for himself:

> Yet still this dream engaged his vanity:
> That could he get upright he would dance and cry
> Shame on every shy or idle wretch.

The ultimate value of Hughes might be that he had the strength to stand up and endure in the face of violence, to endure while confronting the "gaoler's boot" and the "dog's fang." In a role that sets him apart from Plath and Gunn, he fulfills that famous prescription of Faulkner: "The poet's voice need not merely be the record of man, it can be one of the props, the pillars to help him endure and prevail."[16] The Nobel prize winner had envisioned the difficulties of writing of the inner life when the pressures of the outer life become overwhelming:

There are no longer problems of the spirit. There is only the question: When will I be blown up. Because of this, the young man or woman writing today has forgotten the problems of the human heart in conflict with itself which alone can make good writing because only that is worth writing about, worth the agony and the sweat.[17]

Hughes might have been conscious of this sentiment while writing "A Woman Unconscious," for in this poem he contrasts the universal destruction ("the world-cancelling black") to the individual death:

> Did a lesser death come
>
> Onto the white hospital bed
> Where one, numb beyond her last of sense,
> Closed her eyes on the world's evidence
> And into pillows sunk her head.

Again and again characters in Hughes's poems are made noble in their endurance. The speaker in "The Hawk in the Rain" is the prototype who asserts life in the face of overwhelming odds:

I drown in the drumming ploughland, I drag up
Heel after heel from the swallowing of the earth's mouth,
From clay that clutches my each step to the ankle
With the habit of the dogged grave . . .
. . . .
. . . I,
Bloodily grabbed dazed last-moment-counting
Morsel in the earth's mouth, strain towards the master-
Fulcrum of violence. . . .

In "November" the tramp who is discovered in the ditch shares the discomfort of situation of both the man in "The Hawk in the Rain" and the prisoner
in "Invitation to the Dance." Even in his unconsciousness, the tramp participates in life to a greater extent than the observer who runs away:

I took him for dead,

But his stillness separated from the death
Of the rotting grass and the ground. A wind chilled,
And a fresh comfort tightened through him,
Each hand stuffed deeper into the other sleeve.

Faulkner, in the speech quoted above, said that man "must teach himself
that the basest of all things is to be afraid." The theme of "November" is
the difference between fear and trust. The animals at the end of the poem
are further extensions of the enduring man:

Some still had their shape,
Had their pride with it . . .
Patient to outwait these worst days.

This endurance in Hughes frequently takes the form of initiation, the
acting out of Conrad's submission. No poem illustrates this as clearly as
"The Conversion of Reverend Skinner." Reverend Skinner avoids the ugly
realities of life by closing his eyes to them, by pretending that they do not
exist. Insolently, he attempts to remove himself from the harlot, "Dare you
reach so high, girl, from the gutter of the street?" But to mortify his pride,
he "swore to live on dog-licks for ten years," during which time he immerses
himself in the most ugly elements of life. From his position in the gutter,
he calls out to the whores, "This is the ditch to pitch abortions in." His
initiation, however, brings knowledge without redemption; he experiences
only destruction until, looking into the black sky, he sees in the fragile
moon a metaphor for the endurance of the human spirit in the face of
devouring darkness:

Then he saw the thin moon staggering through the rough
Wiping her wound. And he rose wild
And sought and blest only what was defiled.

Stephen Spender once wrote, "The greatest modern poet would be the
poet most capable of accepting the most anti-poetic and brutal phenomena
. . . and revealing them as expressions of man's spirit even in being denials
of man's spirit."[18] This description more than adequately sums up Hughes's
achievement among postwar writers. His ability to involve himself with violence and to handle it with an exciting poetic technique distinguishes him
from those contemporaries who retreat to the security of safe traditional
technique and conventional minor themes. His ultimate worth might be
best measured against those other poets, Thom Gunn and Sylvia Plath,
who also investigated the principles of violence but who were either destroyed
or intimidated by that contact. Hughes to this point not only emerges
unscathed, but is able to maintain a vigorous driving commitment to life.
While he sits making his wolf mask, his mouth remains well clamped onto
the world.

5

JOHN WAIN
THE EVASIVE ANSWER

A first reading of the poetry of Gunn, Hughes, and Plath reveals that violence is a central and controlling theme for these poets. Their enduring commitment to this subject almost forces the reader to submit, consciously or unconsciously, to the moral and philosophical foundations of their approach. On the other hand, the poets whose stance I call neohumanistic do not focus on violence as a central concern. Life for them is a continuous display of wonder and glory, and anything (including violence) that tends to detract from this aura comes under attack.

The neohumanistic poet assumes that violence is detrimental to the human condition, and he rejects the possibility that it might have regenerative effects. It is essential to understand the evolution of this poetry, or the reader may quickly find himself bogged down in a murky moral quandary. Undoubtedly, the neohumanistic position is attractive, as it offers moral and psychological security, including an invitation to shelter oneself within the folds of modern liberal thought. But under closer scrutiny, the shelter does not appear impregnable; rather, its defenses eventually becomes its weaknesses.

Historically, humanism has been at the fore, leading the mind wherever human experience dared. Accordingly, we might expect neohumanistic poetry to be the most engaged of the poetry dealing with violence. But instead of reacting with understanding, imagination, and daring in defining man's relation to his own nature as well as to his environment, these poets exhibit a moral, and perhaps emotional, immaturity when they approach this subject. Their advice to escape from or to rise above all violence rings false and removes their poetry further from life than does the animal poetry of Hughes. Instead of expanding the boundaries of imagination and experience, these poets expend their energy chiefly in retrenching and fortifying older positions. Humanism has traditionally challenged those institutions which impede man's potential for full realization of his nature, and it does grave harm to have intellectual reaction posturing in humanistic garb. The poets who write from this position have many targets, and therefore it is more difficult to examine their poetry with the same consistency as we have the poets in the preceding chapters. Instead of looking at a number of poems by various authors who seem to be connected by one philosophical viewpoint, I believe it better to proceed with the poetry of a single author, as there is less temptation to force together poems of quite independent nature in the same ideological bed. This approach also guarantees a consistency with the approach to authors in the earlier pages and allows the reader to sort out for himself with greater ease the concepts presented here.

I have chosen to discuss the poetry of John Wain because he has written of violence more than occasionally. He has also made statements outside his poetry that reveal an interest in the subject deeper than that of other neohumanistic writers. The proper place to begin a study of Wain's poetry is with the examination of his basic premise: human goodness and love shall outlast violence and brutality. He is willing to admit to man's instinctive selfishness (Hughes's essential theme), but human interaction ultimately transcends and overcomes petty individual inadequacies.Wain traces the source of the violence in the world to mechanization, industrialization, and the consequent dehumanization of modern society. Western civilization, he says, no longer breeds loving, feeling individuals but automatons who, having lost their identity, are ready to pass on to others the psychological violence of which they themselves are victims. Violence breeds greater violence, and the destructive forces that are loose in the world must be brought under control. Finally, he examines the artist's role in a world of violence. In a predictably evasive manner, he insists that the artist must not escape from his responsibilities by submission to the forces of destruction, but must rise above the violence and in this way withstand the onslaught of the darkness.

Again and again it is evident that poems written from the neohumanistic conviction are means of escape rather than of confrontation. As if in answer to those poets who have commited themselves with more abandon, these poets see small hope for those who struggle against violence. At the most, one can be utterly defeated in the confrontation; at the least, he can suffer moral and psychic paralysis. The neohumanists make the careful distinction between the human and the natural world, a distinction Hughes continually tries to negate. The violence of the natural world is not disturbing unless it encroaches upon the human world. This belief leads to what is perhaps the most damning assumption made by these writers, that violence is the property of the mean, the poor, the ignorant. Because low men are closer to the natural world, they are also closer to violence. It is the intellectual above all who must avoid the violence, because he, living in the noble mind, has the most to lose. Accordingly, the poet believes himself to be in the greatest danger, and his poetry becomes his defense against capitulation. It is a theme that was heard frequently earlier in this century in the poetry of Yeats and Eliot, and for many of us it is the most disturbing quality of their poetry. But Eliot and Yeats, even in their wrongheadedness, frequently bring us closer to understanding. With the poetry presently under discussion, I feel there is no real desire for new insights, or new understanding of violence, but only an intellectual evasion of its implications.

John Wain assumes the role of spokesman for the neohumanistic position with some vigor both in his poetry and in his critical remarks. He has made it quite clear that he considers those poets who are searching into the secret recesses of the psyche in an attempt to come to terms with the modern consciousness inferior to those whose assumptions about human nature are more stable and who are thus able to suggest cures for the illness: "Authors fall into two categories, broadly speaking: those whose concern with humanit is analytical and enquiring, and those who are out to *recommend* something positive."[1] But upon reflection, we find ourselves asking if this is really true; why should these two categories be mutually exclusive? Cannot, or should not, inquiry and analysis be the basis for one's recommendations? While the primary movement of the poetry of Ted Hughes is "analytical and enquiring," he certainly makes positive recommendations for bringing consciousness once again into harmony with instinctual nature. The fault then lies not with Wain's humanism but with the narrow and crippling limitations he imposes upon it. He carries this to such a point that he accuses those who hold skeptical or cynical attitudes towards the modern world of inventing their pessimism:

And this calls into being a special kind of intellectual nuisance: the crusading modernist who is prepared to jump down ten stairs even if he has to dig a pit to do it. There he is, out of sight below ground-level in his pit, but his voice can be heard continually, making the same querulous demand to the rest of us to get our spades and do some digging.[2]

Unlike the poets discussed earlier, Wain does not exhibit a continuing evolution of theme from his early poetry to his later. His style, on the other hand, developed markedly in *Wildtrack* (1965) and *Letters to Five Artists* (1970). In the poetry of Gunn and Hughes, the style and technique are shells in which the poet at times hides unpleasant ideas; Wain, however, seems to use an expanding style to compensate for a static, overburdened theme. The lesson is not difficult to perceive: the inquiry and analysis that

Wain rejects are exactly the approach that would enable the poet to reassess his position continuously, to extend his style along with his ideas, and to confront and challenge the problems of a society that refuses to stand still long enough for the artist to take a narrowly moralistic position against it.

The title poem of Wain's 1956 volume of poetry, *A Word Carved on a Sill*, has its source in a line of Robert Graves. Graves's poem "End of Play" accentuates the persistence of human goodness and love before the onslaughts of brutality and violence:

> Yet love survives, a word carved on a sill
> Under antique dread of the headsman's axe.

The victory of humanity over violence becomes a major theme in Wain's poetry, and he sees the vocal assertion of the human element over everything else as a primary function of the artist: "The artist's function is always to *humanize* the society he is living in, to assert the importance of humanity in the teeth of whatever is currently trying to annihilate that importance."[3] The early poems of *A Word Carved on a Sill* show the poet striving to write according to this prescription.

"When It Comes" grew out of the frenzy of the mid-fifties when the fear of nuclear annihilation drove many in England and America to build their own private bomb shelters. Although there are good descriptions of that final scene of destruction ("When all the mountains crash like kettledrums"), the poet's emphasis is upon the assertion of noble thoughts as man is being annihilated:

> I hope to feel some pity when the knife
> Plunges at last into the world's sick heart
> And stills its pounding and its seething strife:
>
> Mainly for those who never got a start. . . .

These lines illustrate a major failing in Wain's humanistic stance, for while expressing sentiments of private compassion, they fail to come to terms with the situation at hand. The poet's emotions are not directed towards the violence and savagery that is visited upon the hundreds of thousands of suffering human beings, but he thinks of those who are not yet born, those who will never have to suffer. Although our first response might well be, "What a compassionate man this poet is!" the tone of the poem suggests that its object is not the suffering of others, but the ennobling of the self through high-minded thoughts in the face of death.

"Patriotic Poem" presents a similar, but less apocalyptic, view of war. England is not destroyed but "beaten flat by bombs and water." The forces of violence are seen as ineffective against the ennobled human spirit reinforced by patriotic concerns. But Wain again reneges somewhat on his commitment, for in this triumph of humanity over the base powers of war, the people surrender an element of their individuality to their country:

> Rises the living breath of all her children;
> And her deep heart and theirs, who can distinguish?

The repetition of such sentiments as this soon degenerates into humanistic doggerel, and the humanism runs very thin. He attempts to elevate humanity in both these poems, but the price ultimately is too high. It is usually at the cost of some greater virtue that he is able to extol the lesser.

This compromise is unfortunate, for at times Wain achieves a remarkable poetic insight into the psychic violence of the modern condition. "To a Friend in Trouble" brings together elements found in Gunn and Plath in an effective fusion. The loss of love in this poem is traced to the loss of other values, and this relation is expressed in a series of violent images:

> On those sharp edges of your broken love
> You cut your veins, which do not leak out blood,
> But suck in trouble, trouble, to your heart. . . .

Man is obviously the taker here, not the giver, and his introversion and selfishness is traced to greater movements:

> What can I say? except that all about us
> I see a time of melting, a time of unloosing;
> . . . .
> So many faiths dry up or slide away. . . .

As a result, the loss of love is not a personal event but one in which all who live in the modern world share:

> Now all our hearts, I think,
> Suck in this scalding drug through broken veins,
> This dry, ammoniac, destructive pain.

Wain rises to greater compassion in this poem than in "When It Comes" because he admits his own helplessness and participation in the selfishness of the world without becoming self-indulgent. He fully feels the pain of this broken love because he foresees its possible infringement on his own life:

> And in these throbbing nights I also see
> Those broken edges in my doubtful dreams.

This poem is held together by a fine tension exemplified by the ambiguous role of the speaker as both observer and participant. But Wain does not often lower himself to the role of participant; he is more frequently seen as the detached observer making moral judgments upon the world. It is in this position that he undoes the fine touches of a poem like "To a Friend in Trouble." The moralizer is all too present in "This above All Is Precious and Remarkable":

> This above all is precious and remarkable,
> How we put ourselves in one another's care,
> How in spite of everything we trust each other.

The unpoetic nature of the language reflects the emphasis on message rather than on experience. The theme in this poem is also introverted selfishness: the fishermen, the weatherman, and the radio operator all go about their business for their own individual needs. But the poet is overwhelmed by the ability of these selfish acts to interlard in such a way as to triumph over the violence of nature:

> But how it adds up is that when the terrible white malice
> Of the waves high as cliffs is let loose to seek a victim,
> The fishermen are somewhere else and so not drowned.

This moral fable should be enough, but in the second from last stanza, the poet explains that this has only been a metaphor for love in which the selfish drives of two individuals result in mutual love and trust:

> They are simply examples of well-known types of miracle,
> The two of them,
> That can happen at any time of the day or night.

Very apparent here is the direct thematic contrast with Hughes, who saw that man would become most fully human through the acts to which his deeper nature prompted him. Wain sees it as a "miracle" for humanity to rise above this element of his nature and to achieve nobility in spite of those ties that drag him down.

Mechanization is a visible projection of those inner forces that do violence to man's nature. Wain shares with Plath and Hughes a contempt for this aspect of modern culture:

Today the adversary is the machine; having surrounded ourselves with mechanisms that are miracles of precision and refinement, we have become so lost in contemplation of them that all our thinking has become mechanistic. Our ambition is to become machines—then we shall be certain of the very best of everything.[4]

He traces the effects of a mechanized culture in the dehumanization and loss of identity that finally culminate in violent action. In "Music on the Water" he draws a delicate line between the exploitation of the African blacks, the virtual annihilation of the American Indians, and the final full mechanization of America:

> The Indians were gone
> taking with them their music of silence:
> now the black backs bent low, and the long dark song
> moved out across the water:
>
> sound of steamboat, of hammer and saw,
> of locomotives, of clopping horses
> and of the song of sorrowful memory,
> the sound of unknown Africa.

America, in replacing human values with mechanized values, has been transformed from a land of peace to a land of violence: "the American earth, no longer Eden."

In *Wildtrack* Henry Ford and Stalin are equated as the two monstrous heralds of modern life who were willing to sacrifice humanity to the machine

> Henry is my darling,
> And I'm his Model T.
> . . . .
> I'll let him lay me on his line
> And standardize each part:
> I'll double his production with
> The love that's in my heart.

This echoes one of Plath's themes, that normal sexual intercourse has been subsumed by sterile mechanization. In Russia, Stalin fed the peasants to the machine of progress:

> He has invented a nature for himself.
> He has abandoned his limpid Georgian name
> and commanded that they call him *Stalin*, steel.
> . . . .
> It is the nature of steel to beat them down:
> it is the nature of steel to chew their flesh,
> to flatten them, to cut them into shapes
> that can be fitted to the great machine.

The violence that is now so often the handmaiden of society is viewed as a destructive force, and Wain's theme is parallel to Hannah Arendt's, that violence can only lead to greater violence. Hughes foresaw this as well, except that he viewed man's violent response as a positive force, as a valiant struggle to hold on to his vital powers. Wain, of course, sees man's growing involvement with violence as dangerous not only to the nobility of the human spirit but to that spirit's very existence.

Two of Wain's most impressive poems explore violence as a destructive force from which the world must turn away. "A Song about Major Eatherly" and "On the Death of a Murderer" trace the disintegrating effects that violence has, not upon its victims, but upon those who initiate such action and also upon those who observe it. Violence is seen as a chain of reaction whose destructive effects cannot be stopped once set in motion.

"A Song about Major Eatherly" examines the gradual metamorphosis into a madman of the man who supposedly piloted the plane that dropped the bomb on Hiroshima. "Good news," says the poet, "It seems he loved them after all." Major Claude Eatherly, according to a report in *The Observer* that Wain quotes at the beginning of the poem, at first was subject to extreme nervous depression and was given a pension of $237 a month. He looked upon it as blood money, however, and "took to petty thievery, for which he was committed to Forth Worth prison." The "good news" is that Major Eatherly took upon himself the moral burden of his actions and rescued himself from the greater spiritual destruction. In piloting the plane that carried such devastation to its goal, he had resigned his humanity, for he had allowed himself to be used as an instrument rather than as a man:

> His orders told him he was not a man:
> An instrument, fine-tempered, clean of stain,
> All fears and passions closed up like a fan:
> No more volition than his aeroplane.

In his acceptance of guilt, "he fought to win his manhood back," for the destructive act is as harmful to the destroyer as to the victim:

> To take life is always to die a little: to stop
> any feeling and moving contrivance, however ugly,
> unnecessary, or hateful, is to reduce by so much the total
> of life there is. And that is to die a little.

There is, however, danger in this acknowledgment, for those who had earlier seen this action as a great patriotic act now must respond out of guilt, for in accepting himself as guilty, Eatherly is also pointing a finger at that society that produced and supported his actions. He the destroyer then becomes a victim in his own society:

> A murderer hides the dead man in the ground:
> but his crime rears up and topples on to the living,
> for it is they who now must hunt the murderer,
> murder him, and hide him in the ground; it is they
> who now feel the touch of death cold in their bones.

Eatherly's atonement is not a symbolic act. He is no scapegoat, for his repentance does not take away the common guilt; it rather increases it and calls forth greater violence in his hostile imprisonment:

> ... this is penitence for its own sake, beautiful,
> uncomprehending, inconsolable, unforeseen.

The emotions that Wain expresses in this poem are easy to participate in, almost too inviting. And such emotions are exceedingly difficult to attack from a humanistic standpoint. However, it is precisely at this point that we can show why and how the neohumanistic response to violence is evasive. William Bradford Huie's book *The Hiroshima Pilot* exploded the myth that Eatherly piloted the plane that dropped the bomb and later was driven to self-destructive criminal acts through guilt for his part in the bombing. In reality, Eatherly commanded the advance weather plane (he was far away from Hiroshima when the bomb was dropped), and his conversion to pacifism grew more out of his earlier psychological problems that were intensified by his deep resentment that he was not given any publicity or fanfare for his role in the Hiroshima bombing than from a sense of profound moral guilt. As Huie himself noted about the distortion of the Eatherly story, "Hiroshima is the symbol of man's predicament in the Age of Angst (anxiety); and because they, too, feel guilty, many men yearn to hear a profession of guilt."[5] Wain is not guilty of purposefully distorting the truth, but I believe it exposes a humanistic laziness in his overall mentality, that in finding a mythologized story that fits his moral outlook, he adopts that as fact and uses it as a moral sledgehammer.

Again and again the poem is marred by the poet's compulsion to philosophize and moralize, as though he were unable to make his point through mere presentation. The third section of fifty-six lines is historical moralizing that detracts from what is in other areas an impressive poem. And at the very end the poet shows that his sympathies are neither with Major Eatherly nor with the society that he represents; the humanizing impact, which he imposes upon the reader too energetically, is that the bomber pilot has taught us to reject violence:

> But lay a folded paper by his head,
> nothing official or embossed, a page

torn from your notebook, and the words in pencil.
Say nothing of love, or thanks, or penitence:
say only "Eatherly, we have your message."

Another poem that grew out of the experience of World War II and presents a moral comment on the effects of the war is "On the Death of a Murderer." As the title suggests, it is a homily that traces the continuous chain of violence and cruelty that the war set in motion. The opening lines describe in effective cadences both birth and death: the death of the Nazi soldier and the values he represented; the birth of a new cruelty and lack of pity that his murderers precipitate:

> Over the hill the city lights leap up.
> But here in the fields the quiet dusk folds down.

As in the preceding poem, the hunter in war has become the hunted; he is tracked down like an animal and "lies in a ditch . . . the voices of his hunters, coming nearer."

This scene is interrupted after the first stanza to describe the Nazi soldier's background. He was the product of a sick and desperate society: "born in Germany, thrashing like a fish / On a gravel towpath beating out its life." This cultural sickness was reflected in childhood illness that "nearly strangled him with impersonal cold fingers." Although he survived, it was only a reprieve, for later in life those fingers would clutch him again.

He grew up in the Berlin streets and learned the bitterness of life at first hand, "while English schoolboys chalked / Dirty words and sniggered behind desk lids." The hate that he learned at an early age he would teach to the rest of Europe, for the fruit of violence is greater violence, of hatred, greater hatred:

> Now his hate has jingled in the ears of Europe.
> He has taught them to know the refusal of pity.
> . . . .
> In a moment they will tear him to pieces.

Hatred and violence are not spontaneous, but they are bred and nurtured over long periods of time. Just as the Nazi soldier is both hunter and hunted, he has been neither the beginning nor the end in the continuing chain of violence. Having been bred by a sick culture, he inspires his murderers to a continuation of that sickness.

As in *Wildtrack* and in "Major Eatherly," society dehumanized the young Nazi in order to make him an instrument of violence. In giving him a gun and whip, it was subverting his sensitivity:

> . . . his gun
> Was a friend, but when they gave him a whip
> He loved that better still.

His education was progress towards dehumanization:

> He fed his starving heart with cruelty
> Till it got sick and died. His masters applauded.

Finally he no longer showed any signs of being human–he is the perfect product of a diseased culture. Even the cruelty and ferocity of his acts are animal rather than human: "Once, he dragged off a man's lower jaw."

Through this history of the soldier, Wain has provided sufficient evidence for his theme. But rather than present the chain of violence through action, he makes his poem a moral conference room and makes his reader sit for the entire lecture:

> But let us watch the scene with a true eye.
> Arrest your pen, hurrying chronicler.
> Do you take this for a simple act: the mere
> Crushing of a pest that crawled on the world's hide?
> Look again: is there not an ironic light
> In the fiery sky that rings his desperate head?

The death of this murderer will not eradicate the disease, for the same refusal to pity that he lived by is used in destroying him:

> When they wrench his body to pieces, will they hear
> A sigh as his spirit is sucked into the air
> That they must breathe?

And their children will grow up, as the Nazi soldier did, breathing air into their hopeful lungs, their hearts jingling with hate. The disease begins again, strangling the human heart and destroying the innocent child:

> And who shall save them
> If after all the years and all the deaths
> They find a world still pitiless, a street
> Where no grass of love grows over the hard stones?

Aesthetically, the reader feels cheated when Wain the moralizer displaces Wain the poet. Ironically, this occurs without necessity, for as we see in these two poems, both the concepts and the designs are vigorous and imaginative, but it is almost as if the poet had doubts about the effectiveness of his art. The difficulty goes back to Wain's distinction between poets who analyze and inquire, and poets "who are out to *recommend* something positive." In making that distinction, he asserts that inquiring analysis in a poet prevents him from offering solutions, from recommending answers to the problems under his scrutiny. As a result, in a poem like "On the Death of a Murderer," in which Wain himself is the horrified analyst of modern violence, he feels compelled not to let his observation stand on its own merits and he intervenes with offensive nonpoetic explanations and recommendations. Rather than integrate his message into the expressive part of his art, he frequently sets off sections of didactic verse within a poem in order to emphasize his theme. His moral concerns appear to be so great that he fears they may be lost in the artistic process. Certainly we can expect Wain, who has shown himself to be an astute critic in his own right, to be more aware of the relation between propaganda and art, and the necessity for integrating the two; and he should be conscious of how his refusal to subordinate the former to the latter affects his poetry.

It is perhaps this tension in his artistic credo that induces him to write poems about his own art and the art of others. One third of *Weep before God* is a long poem called "A Boisterous Poem about Poetry." A more recent book of poetry, *Letters to Five Artists*, discusses the lives and art of five friends: Bill Coleman, Victor Neep, Elizabeth Jennings, Lee Lubbers, and Anthony Conran. In both these works Wain philosophizes about his own theory of art and poetry, and his recommendations are an obvious defense of his own poetical position. They are more philosophical reflection than poetry, and he continuously praises those who share his own particular view of the creative artist. The sections that interest us here are those in which he discusses the artist's role in a violent world.

"A Boisterous Poem about Poetry" is a response to the malaise of the late 1950s in which many were asserting that British poetry had exhausted itself, that after Auden's self-exile and Thomas's death there was no poet with sufficient vitality and vigor to continue the tradition. Wain suggests that the gloom-mongers were too willing to entomb the spirit of modern poetry:

He calls the corpse of poetry back to life, proclaiming the present era "the greatest of all days / That ever called a poet out to sing." But then, back to his distinctions. There are serious poets and fickle poets, the accomplished and the uninitiated. His distinctions rest upon strange grounds, for it is the

> They fell too promptly into step, and marched
> Behind the hearse of poetry, which swayed
> And rumbled, full of dignity and plumes,
> Piled high with wreaths from children, colleagues, friends.

amateur poet, according to Wain, who concerns himself with the dark side of life: violence, cruelty, sorrow, despair:

> Every life has grief, and grief makes poems.
> It is easy material, fit for beginners.
>
> No novice is without his bag of despair,
> To scatter poem–seeds on the ground,
> And water them freely.

The serious poet, on the other hand, is an ameliorator, who observes an unbalanced situation and sets out to rectify it. In his role as healer and savior, the serious poet is somehow able to call on the hidden resources of language to effect his ends, while the poet with his "bag of despair" can only "rattle on tin cans / And claim that [he is] singing":

> Call in the poet with his puncturing needle,
> His long pragmatical stethoscope, his eye
> Versed in the symptoms of the slogan–pox.
> He has the drug that can burn language clean,
> To make it fit to put into your mouth:
> The greatest antiseptic drug of all,
> Antibiotic, disinfectant, harsh,
> Yet gentle to all rightful skin and flesh.

Wain returns to this theme in "Ferns," in which he compares the artist's role in the world to a hawk hanging over his prey:

> ... you perch above your century's weather
> still as a hawk, waiting for movement to show
> far down among the trembling grass and flowers,
> no less potent than that fierce bird to master
> your fluttering hunger with the hunter's patience. ...

The associations with Hughes's poetry might not be purely coincidental. In "Thrushes" Hughes had marked the connection between the "bullet and automatic purpose" of the birds and the artistic genius of Mozart. The vital forces of the hawk of "The Hawk in the Rain" are also paralleled. Wain however is out of sympathy with Hughes's exaltation of the hawk over the man drowning in the ploughland, and with his somewhat savage description of the artistic genius. After setting up parallels between the hawk and the artist, Wain proceeds to amend and transform them:

> ... yet unlike him in what your gestures show.
> Life, not death, signals from your high stone:

the wish to tend and nourish, not the impatience
to scatter blood amid the scent of flowers.

The duty of the poet is always to affirm life, he says, especially in an age
that condones an attitude of violence towards life. The neohumanist rises
above the storm of violence and separates himself from those poets who
have involved their lives and their art in the turmoil: "Amid the bawling
freak-show one quiet master!" He advises the artistic spirit to remain uninvolved:

> Poet, guard your love. Feed your rooted patience.
> Only such as you will have any good to show
> for these blank, scurrying years. The time of the stone
> is on us now, the life-denying weather
> of dust-storm and mistral. Withstand it, master,
> and may your dreams be garlands of cool flowers.

In "Introductory Poem" to *Letters to Five Artists,* he suggests that the
artist must not be preoccupied with understanding the violence in which
his world is drowning. The poet, like the guitar player Django Reinhart,
is a lyrical recorder who must make others lament and weep over, not
understand, such violence:

> Django, pluck your strings
> for the gipsies who were gassed
> and the gipsies now in England
> herded from their camps
> legislated into despair
> in England now: pluck, pluck
> the taut strings of our hearts.

"Green Fingers" is written to fellow poet Elizabeth Jennings and praises
her for having kept her sense of proportion in an unbalanced age. Although
the pressures of a dark and violent time have been pressing upon her, she
is praised because she has managed to avoid the tensions that such a world
forces upon many sensitive people. Without weighing the merits of Jennings'
poetry, one can easily observe that Wain's later poetry is consistent with
his earlier philosophical assumptions. In fact, it is almost embarrassing in
its lack of development. Even here assessment and analysis are unimportant;
he praises her because she was able to remain untouched by the dark:

> Green–fingered artist, I see you never doubt
> Even in those lost days, denying, stark,
> What is the work that you must be about:
>
> A world of colour blossoming in the dark!

The deficiency in Wain's philosophy is that the major problems of mankind are not confronted, or, if they are, only obliquely. Poetry becomes, from his point of view, an assertion of optimism, a refusal to open one's eyes in the dark. I think immediately of Sylvia Plath and how she plunged her sensibility into the violence of her age and was trampled by those dark horses. Wain's uncompromising humanism demands the affirmative voice even when events might lead elsewhere. By rejecting analysis and inquiry for indiscriminate assertion, his humanism must be seen as less than adequate for our moment. His final observation for Elizabeth Jennings is typical of those who seek evasive answers: "Your art will save your life, Elizabeth." Wain looks with satisfaction upon the artist who uses her art to shield herself from, rather than to involve herself with, life. This final line, with its associative recollections of Sylvia Plath's death, emphasizes the major differences among the poets who are concerned with the violence that finds its expression in the immediate historical context.

In the first chapter of this study, I attempted to show that the violence that is directed against man's mind, against his spirit, in this century, is greater than that directed against his physical nature. The very awareness of man's capabilities for universal destruction constitutes a psychological danger that is as pernicious and destructive as the physical factors. The study of the ramifications of such violence and of the means that man must employ to survive has been the work not only of the sociologist and psychologist, but of the novelist, dramatist, and poet as well. Some see that the individual's only hope of survival is to match institutionalized violence with a display of personal violence. Others warn against surrender to the violent elements in man's nature, and they would have us defuse a situation that is degrading and dehumanizing by recognizing that capitulation to violence only spawns greater disorder and chaos, and ultimately dehumanization. Still others cry with horror that we have moved beyond hope, that there is no way to amend a situation that we have allowed to get beyond our control, and that it is better to be destroyed while asserting our humanity than to be forced to submit and unite ourselves to a violent world.

The most distressing effect of the violence of the 1930s, 1940s and after is evident in the poetry of those who refuse to confront this issue. As mentioned earlier, the main trend in British poetry since the war has been one of retreat. Not since the Georgians had the poetic horizons been so limited. On the one hand, this retreat can be explained as a natural reaction to the metaphysical systems of Eliot and Yeats, the propaganda of Auden, the romantic exuberance of Thomas. But on the other, there seems to be present in the poetry of the 1950s and 1960s a strong psychological reaction to the events of recent history: the Spanish Civil War, the rise of

Stalin, the growth of Nazism and fascism in western Europe, the decline of the British empire. The feeling of the poets was closely akin to Auden's during the Spanish Civil War:

> We are left alone with our day and the time is short and
> History to the defeated
> May say, alas, but cannot alter or pardon.
>
> [*Spain*]

The withdrawal from life especially characterized the two poetical focal points of the 1950s: the Movement and the Mavericks. The former retreated to minor themes couched in carefully structured verse; indeed, their attention to the delicacy of technique was a means of evasion. The Mavericks wrote in a neo-Georgian manner. The feelings of both these groups were well expressed by Patrick Kavanaugh in "Nineteen Fifty-four":

> Nineteen fifty-four hold on till I try
> To formulate some theory about you. A personal matter:
> My lamp of contemplation you sought to shatter,
> To leave me groping in madness under a low sky.
> O I wish I could laugh! O I wish I could cry!
> Or find some formula, some mystical patter
> That would organize a perspective from this hellish
>   scatter—
> Everywhere I look a part of me is exiled from the I.
> Therefore I must tell you before you depart my position;
> Making the statement is enough—there are no answers
> To any real question. But tonight I cannot sleep;
> Two hours ago I heard the late homing dancers.
> O Nineteen Fifty Four you leave and will not listen,
> And do not care whether I curse or weep.

One of the poets who refused to withdraw before these difficulties was Sylvia Plath. Her poetry, rather than providing her with a means of escape, brought her to a greater understanding of the horrors that were present in the world. Hers was not an unwillingness to confront the violence, but the inability to reconcile the inner self with the outer world. The secretary in *Three Women*[6] seems to be speaking for the author herself:

> It is I, It is I—
> Tasting the bitterness between my teeth.
> The incalculable malice of the everyday.

As she arrived at a greater awareness, she found a greater need for the release of tension in her poetry. The struggle that she endured and expressed in her last poetry often occurred in the unreal hours of early morning: "These new poems of mine have one thing in common. They were all written at about four in the morning—that still blue, almost eternal hour before cockcrow, before the baby's cry, before the glassy music of the milkman settling his bottles."[7]

Plath's poetry led her into the darkness from which there was no exit. She is like the man in "Suicide off Egg Rock" who was unable to close his eyes to the unpleasant realities of existence. The wasteland is still with us, she says through the imagery of that poem: the hotdogs that "split and drizzled / On the public grills," "the ochreous salt flats," "gas tanks, factory stacks." What must be remembered of Sylvia Plath is that she had the courage to reproduce her vision of horror in her poetry, that she found an artistic medium for her inner struggle. It is hardly surprising that in a world where loss of identity is coupled with the state's continuing encroachment on individual rights she has been canonized as the prophet of the despairing vision. Young people from many countries have gathered around her in adulation that many say is out of proportion with the quality of her poetry. However, intensity is the most important element of her message, and there is a strange attraction in her finally stated realization that the severing of one's ties with his violent origins is itself an act of violence.

Both Gunn and Hughes see violence as an experience through which man passes towards a greater participation in and understanding of his humanity. More than any of the poets who have been discussed, they have been able to reconcile the inner world of vision with the external world of violence. They fully realize the destructive powers of violence when these forces are directed towards the suppression of our humanity. In *Literature and Psychology* F. L. Lucas has pointed to the necessity of this accommodation: "We master more and more each year the forces of this world we live in; they will only make our destruction the more utter, if we cannot learn to master also the hidden forces within ourselves."[8] Hughes, as I have shown, has surpassed Gunn in exploring the role of violence according to the prescription of Lucas. Hughes shows little interest in the individual expression of violence, but his investigations concern man's very nature. Nor does he indulge in timid moral castigations, as the neohumanists do. Rather than present individual fragments of reality, his poetry has mythic proportions and traces large patterns of behavior. His detachment cannot be seen as disinterestedness in his subject but rather a means to greater understanding. By excluding personality, sentiment, and at times human life, from his poetry, he assures himself of the objectivity and emotional refinement needed for philosophical observation. As a true poet, he is always conscious of the linguistic means at his disposal. Although his language may startle, may force the reader into submission, Hughes is not a propagandist or a sensationalist. When we read his poetry, it is difficult indeed not to be impressed by his full commitment to truth. He is one of the few contemporary poets who look upon the cosmic investigations of Eliot and Yeats with both a sympathetic and emulative eye.

His own attempts to explain adequately the nature of violence both in man and in the world are still very much in progress. Whether he too will find the effort too dangerous, too exhausting in terms of his own humanity is yet to be seen. What seems obvious at this point is that he is not to be destroyed by the confrontation, nor is he to take shelter in arguments of moral superiority. It would be a great loss if he were to retreat from his commitment, or become content with the effort that he has made up until now, for his assertive and forceful investigations are healthy counterparts to the stability and staidness of much of the other poetry of this period.

Besides those poets who retreated to the trivial and banal, violence has affected the consciousness of the neohumanists in the most dangerous way. For these poets, perhaps in overreaction to a world that they find distasteful, have been stripped of their sense of perspective, of proportion. Their evasiveness is not only obvious in their stance of moral superiority, but equally apparent in their grossly exaggerated and horrified reaction to the simplest elements of everyday living. For example, a poem like "Crab" becomes grotesque when the poet associates the preparation of crabs for dinner with the "soft soldier / fried in the cockpit of a tank." These lines illustrate the extremes to which the artist may be driven in his reaction to violence. He has been, we might say, oversensitized to such an extent that he can see in the most commonplace things metaphors for man's violence and cruelty. Poems of this nature, with their sensationalism, their sentimentality, their illogical leaps, are finally a greater comment on the poet than on his subject matter. It shows us to what extent his vision and sensibility have been distorted by the events around him.

Peter Porter, in "Annotations of Auschwitz," shows that he has been affected in a similar way. The violence of Nazi Germany has warped his vision; the slaughter of the Jews causes madness, horror, and shame to infest his life:

> My suit is hairy, my carpet smells of death,
> My toothbrush handle grows a cuticle.
> I have six million foulnesses of breath.

Not only is man's life invaded by these remembrances, but they color his vision of the natural world:

> The frenetic butterfly, the bee made free by work,
> Rouse and rape the pollen pads, the nectar stoops.

The poet is horrified by the reaction of the artist who, in an ironic aesthetic insensitivity, thinks only of the artistic possibilities of the scene of 40,000 skulls in a river, while the common man cares not at all:

> Such death, says the painter,
> Is worthwhile—it makes a colour never known.
> It makes a sight that's unimagined, says the poet.
> It's nothing to do with me, says the man who hates
> The poet and the painter.

Porter might well be responding to those writers who refused to react strongly to the experience of the war, who sought escape through aesthetic detachment. He himself expresses a fear of becoming insensitive, of being made so callous by cruelty and violence that no brutal act will be able to affect him:

> I need never feel afraid
> When I salt the puny snail—cruelty's grown up
> And waits for time and men to bring into its hands
> The snail's adagio and all the taunting life
> Which has not cared about or guessed its tortured scope.

As in "Crab," man has been infected by the violence of his age, and the simplest acts can accuse him of complicity with this violence:

> London is full of chickens on electric spits,
> Cooking in windows where the public pass.
> This, say the chickens, is their Auschwitz,
> And all poultry eaters are psychopaths.

This response seems unbalanced, and prepares the reader to view other poetry that grows out of the same impulse with greater caution and perspective. It helps explain, for example, the poem "The Historians Call up Pain," in which Porter tells how we might escape from pain by ritualizing it in examinations (or in poetry). It explains also Jon Silkin's reaction to the fly's death in "A Death to Us," where he is unable to face the reality of meaningless death, even in such an insignificant creature as a fly, and therefore he compensates for this sense of valuelessness by elevating the fly's death, somewhat ridiculously, in a symbolic ritual:

> So I must give his life a meaning,
>
> So I must carry his death about me
> Like a large fly, like a large frail purpose.

But poetry can be more than the philosophical escape from violence. Whereas Hughes had seen the connection between the creative act and the instinctive murderous act ("Thrushes"), the neohumanist sees his poetry as a purgation of those dangerous tendencies. Poetry for him is not an entrance to the inner recesses of the workings of violence, but the draining off of spirits that might move him in that direction. His poetry becomes, under these circumstances, a substitute for living.

George MacBeth well expresses the purgative nature of poetry in "The Blood-Woman." His note to this poem not only stresses the draining of the bad blood, but also emphasizes the ritual aspects of the act of creation: "In the moment of composition, a poet believes he is waiting for a Muse whose embraces will drain his blood. He relates the vampire-act of poetry to the sacrificial rites of the Aztecs, the conquests of the Norsemen, and the movements of his own body."⁹ Significantly, there are parallels to the ritual tones of Plath's poems (especially "Daddy" and "Lady Lazarus") in which she tries to stave off an encroaching reality. The blood-woman in MacBeth's poem is coming to cleanse an infection through the letting of blood with a needle (the pen):

> I am naked, stripped
> of the sheep and the bull. There is nothing
> but whiteness. The clean room is
> the clean page is the cleared theatre
> where the nun intoning her requiem wilts
> into light. My pencil is broken.
> Here is the needle, the blood-woman.

It is this assurance of stability and sobriety, the smug feeling that their poetry will purge them of unclean thoughts, that we frequently find offensive in these poems. Is the attitude that I have described as neohumanistic the effect of moral arrogance, a genuine fear of confronting the darkness, or simple detachment from the reality of suffering? Christopher Logue in "A Singing Prayer" harshly reproves those who attempt to sidestep the issue of suffering:

> Pay no heed, though you love them,
> To the defeated who shrug at pain,
> Seeking at most a lesser pain.
> Nothing comes of that brave nothing.

Until now, many critics have praised the postwar British poets for their ability to confront life, to deal with the vast issues (Tomlinson) as well as the small (Larkin). But in the tendency outlined in this final chapter, we see a retreat from life in the worst tradition of the poetic ivory tower. It isolates the poet from both past and present, allowing his preconceptions that are perhaps inoperable or ineffective to become substitutes for experience. It is with self-conscious irony that Peter Redgrove describes the sensibility of the neohumanist in terms of a small tipsy animal that is attempting to understand his world:

> He peeps to the tops of moss,
> Chuckles across the small posts,
> Behind a toppled tree nibbles a grass as
> He smashes the glutted surface
> With a great stave of his water,
> Twiddles the sun in it, mutters, mutters
> Poetry, and is at peace.

NOTES

1: LITERATURE AND VIOLENCE

1.   This dichotomy is the basis for Vivian de Sola Pinto's study of modern British poetry, *Crisis in English Poetry: 1880-1940* (New York: Harper, 1958). See especially the first chapter, "The Two Voyages."
2.   Letter to Sir Walter Raleigh appended to *The Faerie Queene.*
3.   "The Study of Poetry."
4.   "Poetry in 1944."
5.   Quoted in *Violence,* ed. Carolyn Sugg (New York: Paulist Press, 1970), p. 45.
6.   *Hitler's Words,* ed. Gordon W. Prange (Washington: American Council on Public Affairs, 1944), pp. 8-9.
7.   *On Violence* (New York: Harcourt, 1970), p. 56.
8.   Ibid., pp. 52, 54.
9.   *Hitler's Words,* p. 11.
10.   *1984* (New York: Harcourt, 1949), pp. 219-20.
11.   Sigmund Freud, *Civilization and Its Discontents* (London: Hogarth Press, 1946), p. 85.
12.   *The Pornography of Power* (Chicago: Quadrangle Books, 1968), p. 79. Rubinoff adapted his title from an article in *Encounter* by Geoffrey Gorer, "The Pornography of Death." Gorer characterizes pornography as "the description of tabooed activities with the purpose of inciting hallucinations or delusions for private enjoyment." The increasing depersonalization of society, or the taboo on individuality, results in a compensation through the pornographic pursuit of power.
13.   Ibid., p. 75.
14.   "After the Tranquillized Fifties," *Critical Quarterly* 6 (summer 1964): 109.
15.   "Violence and Love," *Humanitas* 2 (1966): 206.
16.   M. L. Rosenthal, *The New Poets* (New York: Oxford, 1967), p. 228.
17.   Thom Gunn, "Lines for a Book."
18.   Gunn, "The Beaters."
19.   "Context," *London Magazine,* n. s., 1 (Feb. 1962): 46.
20.   "A New Aestheticism?" *The Modern Poet,* ed. Ian Hamilton (London: Routledge, 1966), p. 164.
21.   "Context," p. 46.
22.   "The Fate of Pleasure," *Beyond Culture* (New York: Viking, 1965), p. 76.

23. Ibid., pp. 76-77.
24. "The State of English Poetry," *Twentieth Century* 168 (Nov. 1960): 438.
25. William Empson, "Autumn on Nan-Yueh."
26. *The Poet Speaks,* ed. Peter Orr (London: Routledge, 1966), p. 168.
27. *Poets of the 1950s,* ed. Dennis Enright (Tokyo: Kenkyusha, 1955), introduction.
28. *New Lines,* ed. Robert Conquest (London: Macmillan, 1956), p. xv.
29. The Movement included a number of younger poets whose poetry appeared in *Poets of the 1950s* and *New Lines.* The latter contained the work of nine poets: Elizabeth Jennings, John Holloway, Philip Larkin, Thom Gunn, Kingsley Amis, D. J. Enright, Donald Davie, Robert Conquest, and John Wain. While far from being homogeneous, they were in common rebellion against cosmic systems and romantic visions, against esoteric symbols and foreign influences. They lowered their sights and their voices in seeking an intelligible, workable poetic expression.
30. *The Modern Poet,* p. 173.
31. *Life and the Poet* (London: Secker & Warburg, 1942), p. 51.
32. John Press, in *The Poet Speaks,* p. 188.
33. *The Pornography of Power,* p. 82.
34. Ibid., p. 95.
35. Quoted by John Harrison in *The Reactionaries* (New York: Schocken, 1967), pp. 88-89.
36. "Context," p. 45.
37. Roy Campbell, "A Letter from the San Mateo Front."
38. *A Vision of Reality* (New York: Barnes & Noble, 1965), p. 207.
39. *The Reactionaries,* p. 128.
40. *On the Boiler* (Dublin: Cuala Press, 1939), p. 20.
41. *The Reactionaries,* p. 128.
42. "English Poetry Since 1945," *London Magazine* 6 (Nov. 1959): 13.
43. *The Demon of Progress in the Arts* (Chicago: Regnery, 1955), p. 97.
44. *Declaration,* ed. Tom Maschler (New York: Dutton, 1958), p. 16.
45. Ibid., p. 87.
46. Ibid., pp. 94-95.
47. Ibid., p. 102.
48. Ibid., p. 20.
49. "The Hero in Search of a Dramatist," *Encounter* 9 (Dec. 1957): 27.
50. "The Writer in His Age," *London Magazine* 4 (May 1957): 46.
51. James Keating, "Interview with William Golding," in *Lord of the Flies,* Casebook edition (New York: Putnam's, 1965), p. 189.
52. E. L. Epstein, "Notes on *Lord of the Flies,*" in *Lord of the Flies,* Casebook edition, pp. 277-78.
53. "The Eccentricity of Alan Sillitoe," *Contemporary British Novelists,* ed. Charles Shapiro (Carbondale, Ill.: Southern Illinois University Press, 1965), pp. 98-99.
54. *Declaration,* p.16.

2: SYLVIA PLATH—THE INTERNALIZED RESPONSE

1. *Poetry: 1900-1965* (London: Faber, 1967), p. 333.
2. See Mary Kinzie, "An Informal Checklist of Criticism," in *The Art of Sylvia Plath,* ed. Charles Newman (Bloomington: Indiana University Press, 1970), pp. 289-91. The author attacks those who have traded too eagerly upon the poet's suicide.
3. Foreword to *Ariel* (New York: Harper, 1966), pp. vii, viii.
4. Robin Skelton, "Britannia's Muse Revisited," *Massachusetts Review* 6 (1965): 834.
5. "After the Tranquillized Fifties," *Critical Quarterly* 6 (summer 1964): 108-9
6. "Context," *London Magazine,* n. s., 1 (Feb. 1962): 46.

7. "English Poetry Today," *Commentary* 32 (1961): 219.
8. *The Poet Speaks,* ed. Peter Orr (London: Routledge, 1966), p. 169.
9. *A Closer Look at Ariel: A Memory of Sylvia Plath* (New York: Harper's Magazine Press, 1973), pp. 42–43.
10. *The Poet Speaks,* p. 171.
11. "Notes on the Chronological Order of Sylvia Plath's Poems," *Tri-Quarterly* 7 (fall 1966): 82.
12. Ibid., p. 84.
13. *The Poet Speaks,* p. 172.
14. *Atlantic Monthly,* Jan. 1957, p. 65.
15. Sylvia Plath, "Ocean 1212-W," *Listener,* 29 Aug. 1963, p. 312.
16. Ibid., p. 312.
17. Ibid., p. 313.
18. Ibid., p. 313.
19. *The New Poets* (New York: Oxford, 1967), p. 87.
20. *The Poet Speaks,* p. 169.
21. Foreword to *Ariel,* p. vii.
22. A. E. Dyson, "On Sylvia Plath," *Tri-Quarterly* 7 (fall 1966): 80.
23. *On Violence,* p. 80.
24. A. Alvarez, "Sylvia Plath," *Tri-Quarterly* 7 (fall 1966): 72.
25. Peter Davison, "Inhabited by a Cry: The Last Poetry of Sylvia Plath," *Atlantic Monthly,* Aug. 1966, p. 77.
26. Jan B. Gordon, "Who Is Sylvia?" *Modern Poetry Studies* 1, no. 1 (1970): 27.
27. Compare Gunn's poem "The Paralytic Lying on His Back," in which the paralytic comes to realize the value of violent action: "That action only is action's end."
28. A. Alvarez quotes these lines of Sylvia Plath in "Sylvia Plath," 67. The quotation is from the introductory notes to "New Poems," a reading prepared for the BBC Third Program but never broadcast.

3: THOM GUNN—THE RETREAT FROM VIOLENCE

1. "The Poetry of Thom Gunn," *Critical Quarterly* 3 (1961): 367.
2. Philip Booth, review of *The Sense of Movement, Christian Science Monitor,* 14 May 1959, p. 14.
3. "Letter from Cambridge," *London Magazine* 1 (Aug. 1954): 69.
4. Frederick Grubb, *A Vision of Reality* (New York: Barnes & Noble, 1965), p. 207.
5. *Poets of the 1950s,* ed. D. J. Enright (Tokyo: Kenkyusha, 1955), introduction.
6. Compare these sets of couplets from the two poems:

    Thomas: "Dead men naked they shall be one
                With the man in the wind and the west moon."

    Gunn: "Cell upon cell the plants convert
                My special richness in the dirt."

7. Alan Brownjohn, "The Poetry of Thom Gunn," *London Magazine,* n. s., 2 (March 1963): 52.
8. Letter of Thom Gunn in *London Magazine* 4 (June 1957): 66.
9. "Four Young Poets–Thom Gunn," *Times Ed. Supplement,* 3 Aug. 1956, p. 995.
10. Gunn's first volume, *Fighting Terms,* in which he is most fully preoccupied with violence, was published in 1954. Ted Hughes, who was the next poet of the same generation to commit himself to this subject with as much vigor, published his first volume of poetry, *The Hawk in the Rain,* in 1957.
11. "It may well be that the 'Movement' anthology–and some of the principles upon which it was put together–provided a springboard for the more adventurous progress of at least two poets [Gunn and Davie] who have in their different ways outgrown or

transformed whatever was provincial and limiting in its aims." Patrick Swinden, "Old Lines, New Lines: The Movement Ten Years After," *Critical Quarterly* 9 (1967): 359.

12.   "Context," *London Magazine*, n. s., 1 (Feb. 1962): 40.
13.   Review of Empson's *Collected Poems, London Magazine* 3 (Feb. 1956): 75.
14.   "The Fate of Pleasure," *Beyond Culture* (New York: Viking, 1965), p. 85.
15.   In addition, the poet uses his intricate metaphors and strict technical forms as types of masks to remove the poem both from himself and from personal emotion. The poems that are characterized by insensitive characters, harsh themes, and complex metaphors appear in Gunn's early work. Martin Dodsworth, in *Review* 18 (April 1968): 46–61, has made a valid case for the body of Gunn's poetry moving from reflections of reality (mask and pose) towards reality itself. In the later volumes, *Positives* and *Touch*, whose titles in fact stress their thematic direction, Gunn communicates his emotions more directly and abandons the pseudomasks of complex and strict technique for less weighty vehicles and freer forms.
16.   *The Writer and Commitment* (London: Secker & Warburg, 1961), p. 161.
17.   "A New Aestheticism?" *The Modern Poet*, ed. Ian Hamilton (London: Routledge, 1966), p. 164.
18.   "Context," p. 40.
19.   Bernard Bergonzi in *The Guardian*, 1 Sept. 1961, p. 5:

> [Gunn] has moved immeasurably far from the forceful but slightly muscle-bound language of his earliest work, and the advance is a question of deepening sensibility as well as of simple increase in skill. . . . I was particularly impressed with a group of poems in the second part of the book, which are unemphatic and apparently free in style but are, in fact, extremely subtle and delicate organisms of language.

20.   Ian Hamilton, "Four Conversations," *London Magazine*, n. s., 4 (Nov. 1964): 65.

4: TED HUGHES—ACCEPTANCE AND ACCOMMODATION

1.   "Dreams and Responsibilities," *The Modern Poet*, ed. Ian Hamilton (New York: Horizon, 1969), p. 10.
2.   Three years separated the publication of *Fighting Terms* (1954) and *The Hawk in the Rain* (1957).
3.   See especially J. D. Hainsworth, "Ted Hughes and Violence," *Essays in Criticism* 14 (1965): 356–59.
4.   "Talking Beasts," *Shenandoah* 19 (summer 1968): 61.
5.   "Dreams and Responsibilities," p. 11.
6.   M. L. Rosenthal, *The New Poets* (New York: Oxford, 1967), p. 228.
7.   "Poetry is not a turning loose of emotion, but an escape from emotion; it is not the expression of personality, but an escape from personality." *The Sacred Wood* (London: Methuen, 1920), p. 58.
8.   *Rule and Energy* (New York: Oxford, 1963), p. 182.
9.   Seneca, *Oedipus*, adapted by Ted Hughes (London: Faber, 1969), p. 8.
10.   *Rule and Energy*, p. 187.
11.   George Orwell used the aspidistra frequently as a symbol of middle class respectability and smugness, most notably in *Keep the Aspidistra Flying*. He also mentions the aspidistra in *The Clergyman's Daughter*, where its ominous connotations are similar to those in this poem: "Women who don't marry wither up—they wither up like aspidistras in back-parlour windows; and the devilish thing is that they don't even know they're withering.' "
12.   We might recall Roy Fuller's fascinated horror of crabs in "Crustaceans." Also, in "Meditation" Fuller sees a parallel between crabs and the destructive intellects of war:

While outside the demon scientists and rulers of the land
Pile up the bombs like busy crabs pile balls of sand.

13.　In "Roan Stallion," California, desiring to be absorbed by the power of the stallion, cries,

"But I will ride him
Up into the hill, if he throws me, if he tramples
me, is it not my desire
To endure death?"

14.　*Fantasia of the Unconscious* (New York: Seltzer, 1922), pp. 154–55.
15.　*The Rainbow* (New York: Random House, 1915), p. 462.
16.　*The Nobel Prize Speech* (New York: Spiral Press, 1951), unpaginated.
17.　Ibid.
18.　*Life and the Poet* (London: Secker & Warburg, 1942), p. 51.

5: JOHN WAIN—THE EVASIVE ANSWER

1.　John Wain, "Along the Tightrope," *Declaration,* ed. Tom Maschler (New York: Dutton, 1958), p. 87.
2.　Ibid., p. 95.
3.　Ibid., p. 87.
4.　Ibid., p. 87.
5.　*The Hiroshima Pilot* (New York: Putnam, 1964), p. 290.
6.　*Three Women: A Poem for Three Voices,* produced by Douglas Cleverdon for the BBC Third Program, first transmitted August 19, 1962.
7.　This quotation is from the introductory notes to "New Poems," a reading prepared for the BBC Third Program but never broadcast.
8.　*Literature and Psychology* (London: Cassell, 1951), p. 19.
9.　*The Color of Blood* (New York: Atheneum, 1967), p. 79.

BIBLIOGRAPHY

GENERAL

Alvarez, A. "English Poetry Today." *Commentary* 32 (1961): 217-23.
British Poetry Since 1960: A Critical Survey, ed. Michael Schmidt and Grevel Lindop. Oxford: Carcanet Press, 1972.
Cox, C. B. and Jones, A. R. "After the Tranquillized Fifties." *Critical Quarterly* 6 (summer 1964): 107-12.
Declaration, ed. Tom Maschler. New York: Dutton, 1958.
Fraser, G. S. "English Poetry Since 1945." *London Magazine* 6 (Nov. 1959): 11-36.
Grubb, Frederick. *A Vision of Reality.* New York: Barnes & Noble, 1965.
Mander, John. *The Writer and Commitment.* London: Secker & Warburg, 1961.
The Modern Poet, ed. Ian Hamilton. New York: Horizon, 1969.
New Lines, ed. Robert Conquest. London: Macmillan, 1956.
Pinto, Vivian de Sola. *Crisis in English Poetry: 1880-1940.* New York: Harper, 1958.
The Poet Speaks, ed. Peter Orr. London: Routledge, 1966.
Poetry: 1900-1965, ed. George MacBeth. London: Faber, 1967.
Poets of the 1950s, ed. D. J. Enright. Tokyo: Kenkyusha, 1955.
Press, John. *Rule and Energy.* New York: Oxford, 1963.
Rosenthal, M. L. *The New Poets.* New York: Oxford, 1967.
Skelton, Robin. "Britannia's Muse Revisited." *Massachusetts Review* 6 (1965): 834-35.
Swinden, Patrick. "Old Lines, New Lines: The Movement Ten Years After." *Critical Quarterly* 9 (1967): 347-59.
Williams, Christopher. "The State of English Poetry." *Twentieth Century* 168 (Nov. 1960): 436-42.

INDIVIDUAL POETS

THOM GUNN

(Individual Works)

Fighting Terms. London: Fantasy Press, 1954; London: Faber, 1962, rev. ed.
A Geography. Iowa City: Stone Wall Press, 1966.
Moly. London: Faber, 1971.
My Sad Captains. Chicago: University of Chicago Press, 1961.
Poems: 1950-1966. London: Faber, 1969.
Positives. Photographs by Ander Gunn. Chicago: University of Chicago Press, 1966; London: Faber, 1966.
The Sense of Movement. London: Faber, 1957; Chicago: University of Chicago Press, 1959.
Touch. London: Faber, 1968; Chicago: University of Chicago Press, 1968.

(Essays, interviews, etc.)

"Correspondence." *London Magazine* 4 (June 1957): 65–66.
"Context." *London Magazine,* n. s., 1 (Feb. 1962): 27–53.
"Letter from Cambridge." *London Magazine* 1 (Aug. 1954): 66–69.
Review of William Empson, *Collected Poems. London Magazine* 3 (Feb. 1956): 70–75.

(Critical Reviews)

Booth, Philip. Review of Thom Gunn, *The Sense of Movement. Christian Science Monitor,* 14 May 1959, p. 14.
Brownjohn, Alan. "The Poetry of Thom Gunn." *London Magazine,* n. s., 2 (March 1963): 45–52.
Dodsworth, Martin. "Thom Gunn: Negatives and Positives." *Review* 18 (April 1968): 46–61.
"Four Young Poets: Thom Gunn." *Times Ed. Supplement,* 3 Aug. 1956, p. 995.
Fraser, G. S. "The Poetry of Thom Gunn." *Critical Quarterly* 3 (1961): 359–67.
Fuller, John. "Thom Gunn," in *The Modern Poet,* ed. Ian Hamilton. New York: Horizon, 1969.
Hamilton, Ian. "Four Conversations." *London Magazine,* n. s., 4 (Nov. 1964): 64–70.
Miller, John. "The Stipulative Imagination of Thom Gunn." *Iowa Review* 4, no. 1 (winter 1973): 54–72.

TED HUGHES

(Individual works)

The Burning of the Brothel. London: Turret Books, 1966.
Crow: From the Life and Songs of the Crow. New York: Harper, 1971.
Five Autumn Songs for Children's Voices. Bow, Devon: Richard Gilbertson, 1969.
The Hawk in the Rain. London: Faber, 1957; New York: Harper, 1957.
Lupercal. London: Faber, 1960; New York: Harper, 1960.

Recklings. London: Turret Books, 1966.
Scapegoats and Rabies. London: Poet and Printer, 1967.
Season Songs. New York: Viking, 1975.
Selected Poems: 1957-1967. New York: Harper, 1972.
Wodwo. New York: Harper, 1967; London: Faber, 1967.

(Essays, interviews)

"Context." *London Magazine,* n. s., 1 (Feb. 1962): 27-53.
"Notes on the Chronological Order of Sylvia Plath's Poems." *Tri-Quarterly* 7 (fall 1966): 81-88.

(Critical reviews)

Bedient, Calvin. "On Ted Hughes." *Critical Quarterly* 14 (summer 1972): 103-21.
Criticism in Action, ed. Maurice Hussey. London: Longmans, 1969.
Faas, Egbert. "Ted Hughes and Crow." *London Magazine,* n. s., 10 (Jan. 1971): 5-20.
Hainsworth, J. D. "Extremes in Poetry: R. S. Thomas and Ted Hughes." *English* 14 (1963): 226-30.
———. "Ted Hughes and Violence." *Essays in Criticism* 15 (1965): 356-59.
Hoffman, Daniel. "Talking Beasts: The 'Single Adventure' in the Poems of Ted Hughes." *Shenandoah* 19 (summer 1968): 49-68.
Libby, Anthony. "Fire and Light: Four Poets to the End and Beyond." *Iowa Review* 4 (spring 1973): 111-26.
Rawson, C. J. "Ted Hughes: A Reappraisal." *Essays in Criticism* 15 (1965): 77-94.
Sagar, Keith. *The Art of Ted Hughes.* New York: Cambridge, 1975.
———. *Ted Hughes.* Harlow: Longman for the British Council, 1972.

SYLVIA PLATH

(Individual works)

Ariel. London: Faber, 1965; New York: Harper, 1966.
The Colossus and Other Poems. London: Heinemann, 1960; New York: Knopf, 1962; London: Faber, 1967.
The Bell Jar. New York: Harper, 1971.
Crossing the Water. London: Faber, 1971; New York: Harper, 1971.
"The Goring." *Arts in Society* (fall 1959): 66.
"Ocean 1212-W." *Listener,* 29 Aug. 1963, pp. 312-13.
"Pursuit." *Atlantic Monthly,* Jan. 1957, p. 65.
Three Women: A Poem for Three Voices, produced by Douglas Cleverdon for the BBC Third Program, first transmitted 19 Aug. 1962.
Uncollected Poems. London: Turret Books, 1966.
Winter Trees. London: Faber, 1971; New York: Harper, 1973.

(Critical reviews)

Alvarez, A. *The Savage God: A Study of Suicide.* New York: Random House, 1971.

———. "Sylvia Plath." *Tri-Quarterly* 7 (fall 1966): 65–74.

Arid, Eileen. *Sylvia Plath.* New York: Barnes & Noble, 1973.

The Art of Sylvia Plath, ed. Charles Newman. Bloomington: Indiana University Press, 1970.

Davison, Peter. "Inhabited by a Cry: The Last Poetry of Sylvia Plath." *Atlantic Monthly,* Aug. 1966, pp. 76–77.

Dyson, A. E. "On Sylvia Plath." *Tri-Quarterly* 7 (fall 1966): 75–80.

Gordon, Jan B. "Who Is Sylvia?" *Modern Poetry Studies* 1, no. 1 (1970): 6–34.

Hughes, Ted. "Notes on the Chronological Order of Sylvia Plath's Poems." *Tri-Quarterly* 7 (fall 1966): 81–88.

Perloff, Marjorie. "*Angst* and Animism in the Poetry of Sylvia Plath." *Journal of Modern Literature* 1, no. 1 (1970): 57–74.

Smith, Pamela A. "The Unitive Urge in the Poetry of Sylvia Plath." *New England Quarterly* 45 (Sept. 1972): 323–39.

Steiner, Nancy Hunter. *A Closer Look at Ariel: A Memory of Sylvia Plath.* New York: Harper's Magazine Press, 1973.

JOHN WAIN

"Along the Tightrope." *Declaration,* ed. Tom Maschler. New York: Dutton, 1958.

Essays on Literature and Ideas. London: Macmillan, 1964.

Feng. London: Macmillan, 1975.

Letters to Five Artists. New York: Viking, 1970.

Preliminary Essays. London: Macmillan, 1957.

Sprightly Running: Part of an Autobiography. New York: St. Martin's Press, 1963.

Weep before God. London: Macmillan, 1961.

Wildtrack. London: Macmillan, 1965.

A Word Carved on a Sill. London: Routledge, 1956.

INDEX